	Exit		
SUPER STORE **FUEL**	**1**	IIIIIII TESCO	**Tesco Super Store, Brent Cross T...** A406 > North Circular Rd. East, then Petrol Station OPEN 24 hours. Facilities at this Super Store include:- Coffee Shop. Dispensing Pharmacy, Cash dispenser. Baby changing and t...
B&B	**6**		**The Old Schoolhouse Tel.01727-87...** A405 >St Albans,over M25, R @ roundabout, R @ end of road, 50yds on R, on corner En-suite accommodation in family home. Quiet situation with off street parking. Five minutes walk from town centre & station to London. Good local Services. Each room is centrally heated and has refrigerator, microwave, & colour TV. We strongly advise that you ring ahead.
SUPER STORE **FUEL**	**8**	IIIIIII TESCO	**Tesco Super Store, Hemel Hempstead Tel.01442-239782** A414 >Hemel Hempstead, 1.5m. Petrol Station OPEN 24 hours. Facilities at this Super Store include:- Coffee Shop. Non dispensing Pharmacy, Cash dispenser. Baby changing and toilet
Pub Grub	**9**		**The Wagon & Horses Tel.01582-840079** A5 > Dunstable, 0.5m on R. Open 11-11, Traditional Family Pub, Play facilities, Beer garden.
Pub Grub	**9**		**The Packhorse Tel.01582-841036** A5 > Dunstable, 2m. on L. Open 11-11pm.(Sun 12-3 & 7-10.30) Children welcome, Beer Garden.
Cafe Diner	**9**		**Watling Street Cafe. Tel.01582-840270** A5 > Dunstable, 0.5m on R. Cafe, Diesel. Open 6am close Midnight.Mon-Thurs, close 8.30 Fri. Open weekends.
Pub Grub Restaurant	**9**	BREWERS FAYRE	**Horse & Jockey Tel. 01582 840509** A5 >Dunstable Pub is on the R. (4.2m Off) Our delicious menu provides a wide selection of value for money meals, as well as our own "daily specials". We look forward to welcoming you. Baby changing facilities.Toddler area. Play Zone. Garden. Children's Parties. Outdoor play equipment. Disabled facilities. Accommodation. Breakfasts.
Restaurant	**9**	LITTLE CHEF	**Little Chef Tel.01582-840302** A5 > Dunstable, 1.25 m on R. Open 7am-10pm, Full Little Chef menu.
FUEL	**9**	Shell	**Flamstead Filling Stn. Tel.01582-842098 Fax.842665** A5 > Dunstable 0.5m on R All Fuels, Shop, Toilets, Cafe, Open 24 hours,Sun-Thur, (6.30-10. Fri- Sat)
Hotel	**9**		**The Hertfordshire Moat House Tel.01582-449988 Fax.842282** A5 > Dunstable, 1m on R. *** Modern Hotel, Restaurant, Bar, Body club, near Luton airport.
Pub Grub Restaurant	**10**	BREWERS FAYRE	**Half Moon Tel. 01582 22964** A1081 > Harpenden, 2nd R. Pub is on L after 1m. Our delicious menu provides a wide selection of value for money meals, as well as our own "daily specials". We look forward to welcoming you. Baby changing facilities. Garden. Childrens Parties. Outdoor play equipment.
			REMEMBER – Tiredness kills – TAKE A BREAK

CW01019862

	Exit		
Hotel	**10**		**The Stockwood Hotel Tel.01582-21000** 1st L off the 10a roundabout .7miles on L. Friendly town centre,18 room hotel, residents bar & restaurant. Advise booking.
Relax	**10**		**Stockwood Craft Museum & Gardens Tel;01582-746739 Fax.746763** A1081, Luton, L @ roundabout, follow the brown signs. Country Craft museum & gardens.FREE,Open Tues- Sun, (Winter, Sat & Sun only)
B&B	**10**		**Heritage Halt, 235 Luton Road, Harpenden Tel. 01582-713524** A1081 south to Harpenden (3m) - opp. black & white town sign. Basins/drinks trays in double/family rooms. No smoking. Excellent reputation.
SUPER STORE **FUEL**	**11**	TESCO	**Tesco Super Store, Dunstable Tel.01582-491919** A505 > Dunstable, 0.7m. over roundabout on L (.7m Off). Petrol Station open 6am - Midnight. Facilities at this Super Store include:- Non Dispensing Pharmacy, Cash dispenser. Baby changing and toilets.
Pub Grub	**11**		**Halfway House Beefeater. Tel.01582-609938** A505 > Dunstable, R @ roundabout. All day food, Bar open 11am-11pm,Families welcome, Patio area.
REPAIRS	**11**		**Super Tyres Luton Ltd. Tel.01582-571856 Fax.596995** A505 > Luton, @ r-about return to lights > L, then >R 200 yds. on L. Open 8.30-6.15 (Sun10-1) Tyres, Exhausts, Brakes, Batteries, Clutches
Pub Grub Restaurant	**11**	BREWERS FAYRE	**Old Red Lion Tel. 01582-867439** A505 > Dunstable,turn L to Houghton Regis, then > Toddington.on L (3.5 Off) Our delicious menu provides a wide selection of value for money meals, as well as our own "daily specials". We look forward to welcoming you. Baby changing facilities. Garden. Childrens Parties. Disabled facilities.
Service Area	**S**	Mobil	**Granada, Toddington Services. Tel.01525-875577** Follow the signs Restaurant, Burger King,shop, Barclays & Nat West cash dispenser, Granada Lodge.
REPAIRS	**12**		**Toddington Ford Tel.01525-875177** A5120 > Toddington, 0.75m on R. All Fuels, MOT'S, servicing & repairs.Open 6-9 (Sat 7-7)
B&B	**12**		**B&B @ Pond Farm, Tel.01525-712316** A5120 >Flitwick,> R Greenfield, R @ garage, L @ top of hill, on L.(5m. Off) 17thC arable farm, horses. Hot drinks, TV & basins in all rooms.
Pub Grub	**12**		**The Bell Inn, Tel,01525-712511** >A5120 Flitwick/Ampthill, In village on R. (1.9m. Off) 15 th Century Country Pub with open log fires. No evening meals in winter. We serve home made snacks and meals daily from 12am-3pm and 6pm-10pm. Children very welcome. We have a garden with play equipment.
Cafe Diner	**12**		**Barmy Bites Tel.01525-210969** A5120 > Westoning, 0.5m in layby on L. Mobile Open 7am-3pm. Hot & cold food & all day breakfast.

Please remember to mention "Just Off..."
when you visit one of our locations

Pub Grub	12		**The Angel Inn Tel.01525-872380 Fax.872380** A5120 > Toddington, in village, past the green, opposite shops on L (1.2m Off). Picturesque 16thC Pub and Tea Room serving good English food. This lively pub (CAMRA good pub guide) on the village green at Toddington, has tables outside as well as restaurant and bar. Serves lunches, evening meals, Bar snacks and is Famous for Cream Teas. Coaches please appoint.
Pub Grub	13		**The Bell Tel.01234-768310** A421 > Bedford, R @ roundabout, R @ end of road on the left. (4.5m Off) Victorian village pub with large car park. No smoking dining area serving light bites, starters, grills, home made specials and coffee we have an extensive beer garden with childrens play area Food Served every day, 12-2 & 7-9 (Not Sun.eve.) Coaches please phone.
B&B	13		**The Coach House Tel.01234-767794** A421 > Bedford, R @ roundabout, R @ end of road just past the pub. (4.5 m Off) A converted coach house in old Rectory gardens, En-suite rooms very peaceful.
Hotel	13		**Travel Lodge Tel.0800 850950** A421 > Bedford on the L & roundabout (4 miles) Usual facilities with Little Chef and fuel beside it ETB Lodge commended
Restaurant	13		**Little Chef Tel. 01234-768250** A421 > Bedford on the L & roundabout (4 miles) Usual facilities with Travel Lodge and fuel beside it
Pub Grub Restaurant	13		**Kingston Tavern Tel. 01908-584371** A421 > Milton Keynes, into Standing Way (H8) next to Tesco.(4m Off) Our delicious menu provides a wide selection of value for money meals, as well as our own "daily specials". We look forward to welcoming you. Baby changing facilities.Toddler area. Fun Factory. Garden. Childrens Parties. Outdoor play equipment. Disabled facilities.
Relax	13		**Woburn Abbey Tel.01525 290666** Follow the brown signs off the motorway. Historic House in 3000 acre park. Antique centre. Pottery and Restaurant.
Cafe Diner	13		**Crawley Bunker Stop. Tel;01908-281086** > Woburn 200yds on L. Truck Stop serving food and drinks. Open 7am-Late. (Closed Sun)
Pub Grub cAMPING	13		**Rose & Crown Inn, Tel.01525-280245** A421> Bedford, 1st R > Ampthill, L in Ridgmont 2nd pub on L. Les Routier approved, CARAVAN & CAMPING, meeting rooms,good beer. This 300 year old Inn with it's inglenook fireplace and full of brass, provides hospitality seven days a week with food available every lunchtime and evening. There is a prize winning garden adjoining the camping and caravan park.
Relax	13		**Woburn Safari Park Tel.01525-290407 Fax.290489** Follow the brown signs off the motorway Open March-Oct. An exciting wildlife park with many other attractions.
REPAIRS	13	Q8	**Guise Motors Ltd., Tel.01908-281333 Fax.281327** >A 507 Woburn, 200yds. 24 hour Fuel, workshops breakdown. Avis Car rentals.
FUEL	14	TOTAL	**Petropolis Ltd. Tel.01908-230853** > Milton Keynes, @ 2nd roundabout > M'keynes South, 400yds on L. OPEN 24 hours, All fuels Car wash.

Cafe Diner	**14**		**The Tuck- In Cafe Tel.01908-671242 Fax.670511** > Milton Keynes, 100yds on L. OPEN 24 hours Hot & Cold food at affordable prices. Very friendly atmosphere. Telephones and Toilets on site
B&B	**14**		**The Old Stables Tel.01908-217766 Fax.217766** A509 > Newport Pagnell, 50 yds on R > Moulsoe, 100yds on R. Exclusive B&B. all rooms en suite & TV. Full breakfast. Farm setting.
Service Area	**S**	**Shell**	**Welcome Break, Newport Pagnell Services. Tel.01908-217722** Follow the signs off the motorway Granary self service restaurant, shop, phones, games, and toilets. Little Chef and Travel Lodge, baby change and disabled facilities. Barclays & Nat. West cash. Shell fuels, water & air.
Restaurant	**15**		**A.J's Family Restaurants, Tel.01604-705722** A508 >Northampton, on south bound carriageway. OPEN from 7 am. All facilities, children & disabled welcome.
Hotel	**15**		**Stakis Hotel, Northampton Tel.01604-700666 Fax.792850** A508. Wootton, 300yds on L. All rooms ensuite with mini bars. Sky TV etc.Leisure facilities.
Hotel	**15**	TOBY	**The Midway Toby Hotel Tel.01604-769676 Fax,769523** A508 > Wootton, 1 m >L then > R into car park. Bar & restaurant lunches. Restaurant only evenings. Conference room.
Restaurant	**15**	LITTLE CHEF	**Little Chef Tel.01604-701078** A508 > Wootton, 1m on the L. Open 7am-10pm, Full Little Chef menu. Baby changing & disabled facilities.Fuel.
Service Area	**S**	BP	**Rothersthorpe, Blue Boar Service. Tel.01327-78811** Follow the signs off junction 15a BP Fuel, Diner, Shop, Games.
Pub Grub **Restaurant**	**16**	BREWERS FAYRE	**Cromwell Cottage Tel. 01604-830288** A45 > Northampton, R @ r'bout, on L. (2m Off) Our delicious menu provides a wide selection of value for money meals, as well as our own "daily specials". We look forward to welcoming you. Baby changing facilities.Toddler area. Garden. Disabled facilities. *SPECIAL OFFER*
FUEL	**16**	**Shell**	**P.J.Green Tel.01327-340287** A45 > Daventry, 1.5m on R. Open 7-7.30 (Sat8-6,Sun10-6) All Fuels, Servicing, repairs tyres & groceries.
Pub Grub	**16**		**The White Hart. Tel.01327-340309** A45 > Daventry, 1.5m on L. opposite the garage. Open all day, Families welcome. Real Ale, real clean, real friendly
Pub Grub	**16**		**The Olde Sun Tel.01327-340164** A45 > Daventry, 1st L., 1m in village on L. Traditional English pub with beer patio. Open 12-2 &6-11.
Hotel	**16**		**Heyford Manor Hotel Tel.01327-349022** A45 > Daventry, 1.5m on R. *** Hotel, ensuite rooms with TV & drinks.Mini gym & Sauna, Restaurant

Service Area	**S**	BP	**Watford Gap, Blue Boar Services. Tel.01327-78811** Follow the signs BP. Restaurant. Shop. phone, games and card machines
B&B	**18**		**Paddock Cottage, Tel.01788 823615** A428 > Crick, R @ Co-op, Take the Watford gated Rd. (2.6m.off) Private Facilities, spacious, 2 crowns, commended E.M.T.B.
Hotel	**18**		**Forte Posthouse Tel.01788-822101 Fax.823955** A428 > Northampton, 0.5m on L. Open All Day. Traders restaurant. Leisure & conference facilities.
Pub Grub	**18**		**The Half Way House Tel.01788-822888 Fax.822888** A428 > Rugby, 1st. L Rugby, 0.5m from the Motorway. Open 7am-11pm. Food all day. B&B available.
Pub Grub	**18**		**The Red Lion Inn, Tel.01788-822342** > A428 >Northampton. (0.7m.) Featured in Good Pub, Best Inns & Pubs in the Midlands Guides.
CAMPING	**19**		**Stanford Park Tel. 01788-860387** [N.bound go to 20 & back to 19]. L >Swinford. .5m then R >Stanford Rd. 1m on L. Caravan Club site, open Apl - Oct. (8am - 8pm) No toilets, Shops 1m.
FUEL	**20**	FINA	**Walcote Service Stn. Tel.01455-553911** A427 > Market Harborough, 1m on R. Open 7am-10pm. All Fuels & car wash. Shop with microwave snacks.
Pub Grub	**20**		**The Tavern Inn Tel.01455-553338** A427 > Market Harborough, 1m. in Walcote. Village Free House, hot & cold food to 11pm.Children & Coaches Welcome
Pub Grub **B&B**	**20**		**The Fox Inn Tel.01455-552677 Fax.552677** A427 > Lutterworth > R @ lights 300yds on L. This traditional Pub is renowned for it's Real Ales, Quality food and good service. Sunday lunches are a speciality, There is a double bedded Guest room. Meeting room, and function room. Coaches only by appointment
Hotel	**20**		**Denbigh Arms Hotel Tel.01455-553537 Fax.556627** A427 > Nuneaton, R @ lights, on L in town ***Hotel, Bar, Restaurant, conference room,
Pub Grub Restaurant	**21**	BREWERS FAYRE	**Forest Park Tel. 01162 394677** Leicester ring rd, clockwise, @ A47 r'bout Pub is on L before crossing motorway. Our delicious menu provides a wide selection of value for money meals, as well as our own "daily specials". We look forward to welcoming you. Baby changing facilities.Toddler area. Garden. Childrens Parties. Disabled facilities. Accommodation. Breakfasts.
Hotel	**21**		**Forte Posthouse Tel. 01162-630500** A46 > Leicester, 1.5m > R B5418 on L. *** Hotel, Conference facilities, Bar & Restaurant, all rooms en suite.
SUPER STORE	**21**		**J.Sainsbury Plc.** A46 > Leicester, R @ roundabout, double back @ next roundabout 1st L. OPEN 24 hours. all fuels
Take -away	**21**		**McDonald's Tel.01162-630563** A46 > across roundabout, follow signs to shopping centre.on R. Open 7.30 - 11.30.Full McDonald's menu, Children's tables,

SUPER STORE	21		**Asda Stores Ltd. Tel.01162-898174** A46 > Leicester, across roundabout, > shopping Centre. All Fuels & car wash. Plus super store. Open 7.30-10 pm (Sun 9-6pm).
Cafe Diner	21		**Pizza Hut Tel;01162-892990** A46 > Leicester, R @ roundabout,double back @ next roundabout on L. Full pizza menu, + salad and pasta bar, Licensed Open 12-11pm 7 days.
Service Area	S	BP / LITTLE CHEF	**Welcome Break, Leicester Forest East Services. Tel.01162-386801** Follow the signs off the motorway Granary self service restaurant, shop, phones, games, and toilets. Little Chef, baby change and disabled facilities. Kentucky Fried Chicken restaurant and take- away. BP fuels, water & air.
Pub Grub	22		**The Copt Oak Tel.01530-242353** A50 > Leicester,1st exit on L, > R @ end, 2m. Full menu & Specials Board. Draught beers, Children's menu.
REPAIRS	22		**D.A. Colledge Motor Engineers Tel.01530-245990** A50 > Leicester, 1st L & L at the top of hill.turn R on bend on L. Open 8.30-7.30. Full workshop for repairs. Any make recovery Service.
Hotel	22		**Field Head Hotel Tel.01530-245454 Fax. 243740** A50 > Leicester, 1m > L @ roundabout, 200yds onR. *** Hotel, conference facilities, Bedrooms en suite with Sky TV,Drinks
Service Area	22	Mobil	**Granada, Leicester Markfield Tel.01530-244237** Follow the signs off the motorway. AJ's Family Restaurant, games, shop, Granada Lodge.
Pub Grub Restaurant	23	BREWERS FAYRE	**Bulls Head Tel. 01530-224327** A512 > Ashby de la Zouch, 4 m on L. Our delicious menu provides a wide selection of value for money meals, as well as our own "daily specials". We look forward to welcoming you. Baby changing facilities.Toddler area. Garden. Childrens Parties. Outdoor play equipment. Disabled facilities.
Pub Grub	23		**De Lisle Arms Tel.01509-650170** A512 > Shepshed, 0.5m on L. Open 11.30-2.30 & 5.30-11, Full home cooked menu & Bar snacks.
Hotel	23		**Friendly Hotel Tel.01509-211800 Fax.211868** A512 > Loughborough, 0.5m on L. *** Hotel, Full leisure & Conference facilities, Eat any time of Day.
Cafe Diner Take-away	23		**J 23 T-Bar & Diner. Tel.0585-308809 (mobile)** A512 > Loughborough, 500 yds on L. 24 HOUR SERVICE Good and varied full menu available. hot & cold food and drinks. All day.! We serve Breakfast 24 hours all day every day. Emergency telephone and Toilets.
Cafe Diner	23		**Junction 23 Lorry Park Ltd. Tel;01509-507481 Fax.600667** A512 > Shepshed, 1m on R. Diesel Open 24 hrs. Cafe 6am-9pm Clean & friendly, Chief's Specials.
Take-away	23		**P.J.Catering** A512 Shepshed, 100yds on L. Open 7.30-2pm. Hot Food & All Day breakfasts and drinks.

Pub Grub	23		**The Wheatsheaf Harvester Tel.01509-214165** A512 > Loughborough, 0.5m on L. Open 11-3 &5-11. Modern Pub with Bar & Restaurant.
B&B	24		**Little Chimneys Tel.01332-812458** A453 > Castle Donnington, 2nd L. 0.75 m on L. All rooms en suite, TV,coffee & Tea.
Hotel	24		**Kegworth Hotel Tel.01509-6782427 Fax.674664** A6 > Kegworth, 0.5m on R. *** Hotel, Leisure Club. Restaurant, & Bar.
Pub Grub	24		**Bull & Swan, Grimesgate.** A453 > Castle Donnington, > L to Diseworth village. Open 12-3 & 6-11. Traditional English Pub. Kids welcome,
Hotel	24		**Hilton National Tel.01509-674000 Fax.672412** on the roundabout. Fine modern Hotel with excellent conference facilities.
FUEL	24	ANGLO	**Kegworth Service Stn. Tel.01509-673435** > Kegworth, 0.5m on L Open 7.30-8.30 (7 Days) All fuels, Shop with microwave, Repairs.
Pub Grub	24		**Ye Olde Flying Horse Tel.01509-672253** A6 > Kegworth, 1m on R. Open all day, Family's welcome, Food 12-2 & 6-9
Hotel	25		**Yew Lodge Hotel, Tel.01509-672518 Fax.674730** A6 > Loughborough, 1st R. Packington Hill, on R. Meeting/Conference rooms, RAC/AA. 3 Star, Rooms en suite.TB 4 crown.
Hotel	25		**Sleep Inn Tel.01159-460000 Fax.460726** > Long Eaton, 0.5m on R. Motel style Inn with conference facilities, All rooms en suite with TV
REPAIRS	25	ATS.	**ATS. Tyres & Exhausts Tel.01159-732156** > Long Eaton, R @ island, L @ next island, 1m. over canal & R. Tyres, Exhausts & shock Absorber fitting centre.
Hotel	25		**Novotel Tel.01602-720106 Fax.465900** > Long Eaton, 400yds on L. *** Hotel, outdoor pool, kids stay free, restaurant open 6am-midnight.
Pub Grub	25		**Branaghan's Tel.01159-462000** > Long Eaton, 0.5m on R. beside Sleep Motel. Open 12-3 &5-11pm. Lively American theme bar with full American Menu,
Service Area	S	ESSO	**Granada, Trowell Services. Tel.01602-320291** Follow the signs off the motorway Restaurant, Burger King, shop, toilets, Tourist information.
Pub Grub Restaurant	26		**Old Moor Lodge Tel. 01159-762200** SPECIAL OFFER A52 >Nottingham @ r'bout A6002 > Beeston, on L (1 m Off) Our delicious menu provides a wide selection of value for money meals, as well as our own "daily specials". We look forward to welcoming you. Baby changing facilities.Toddler area. Garden. Childrens Parties. Outdoor play equipment. Disabled facilities.

REMEMBER – Tiredness kills – TAKE A BREAK

Pub Grub	26		**Three Ponds Tel.01159-383170 Fax.382153** > A610 Nottingham, @ roundabout > Watnall in village on L. Open all day, Family play area, Coffee all day, Food 12-2 & evenings.
FUEL	26	BP	**B.P. St. Mary's SISV Tel.o1159-272707** A610 > Nottingham, 1m, double back & 200yds on L. OPEN 24 hours. All Fuels and Car Wash.
Pub Grub	26		**The Broxtowe Inn Tel.01159-278210** A610 > Nottingham, 4th turning on R 800 yds.on L. Open all day, Food 12-2.30 & 5-8.30. Speciality 32oz Steak.
Pub Grub Restaurant	27		**Hole in the Wall Tel. 01773-713936** A608 >Heanor, 2miles, L @ T junction 100yds Pub is signed R .75 m. (3m Off) Our delicious menu provides a wide selection of value for money meals, as well as our own daily specials'. We look forward to welcoming you. Baby changing facilities.Toddler area. Outdoor play equipment. Childrens Parties. Disabled facilities. Accommodation. Breakfasts.
Cafe Diner	27		**Fifth Wheel Snack Bar Tel.01159-639038** A608 > Derby. 100yds on R. Mobile, Open 6-4 Mon-Fri, 6-1 Sat. Drinks, Rolls etc. Breakfasts.
FUEL	28	3D	**Coleman's Garage Tel.01773-811542** A38 > Mansfield, L > S. Normanton, L again on R. Open 8.30-6.(8.30 -12.30 0n Sat.) All Fuels & Garage repair workshop.
Cafe Diner	28		**Billy Bunter's Tel.01773-580842** A38 > Mansfield 200yds on L Open 6-5 Mon-Fri (6-1 Sat.) Mobile with seating hot & cold food served
Take-away	28		**Big Chef Tel.01246-856789** A617 > Mansfield, 0.75m. on the R. Fish & Chips, Kebabs etc, Hot drinks,Open 12-3 & 6-11(not Sundays).
Pub Grub Restaurant	29		**Young Vanish Tel. 01623-810238** A617 > Mansfield, 1 mile on Left. Our delicious menu provides a wide selection of value for money meals, as well as our own "daily specials". We look forward to welcoming you. Baby changing facilities.Toddler area. Garden. Childrens Parties. Outdoor play equipment.
Hotel	29		**Twin Oaks Motel Tel.01246-855455 Fax.855455** > Palterton, immediately on the L. Conference facilities, 23 bedrooms (en suite) Bar snacks & Carvery
Relax	29		**Hardwick Hall Tel.01246-850430 Fax. 854200** Follow the brown signs. Historic Stately Home. Open 1pm - 5pm.Wed,Thur,Sat,Sun.& Bank Holidays Apr.-Oct..
FUEL	29	Shell	**Red House Service Stn. Tel.01246-850329** A6175 > Claycross 0.5m on R. Open early - 9.30pm (8-8 on Sat & Sun) All Fuels Car wash.
Pub Grub Restaurant	30		**De Rodes Arms Tel. 01246-810345** A619 > Worksop, (1 m Off) Our delicious menu provides a wide selection of value for money meals, as well as our own "daily specials". We look forward to welcoming you. Baby changing facilities. Garden. Childrens Parties. Disabled facilities.

	Exit		
Pub Grub	30		**Prince of Wales Tel.01246-423108** A616 > Sheffield, 1.5m. on the L. B & B.Twin bedded rooms. Traditional Pub dated 1890.
REPAIRS	30	**TOTAL**	**Bridge House Garage Tel.01246-810600** A616 > Sheffield, 0.5m on R. Open 7-9 (Sat-Sun 8-8) All Fuels. Full Workshop service & repairs.
B&B	30		**Stone Croft. Tel.01246-810974** A619 > Worksop, L @ roundabout, L @ next roundabout 20yds on R. EMTB 2 crown, Delightful garden, All rooms en suite.
Cafe Diner	30		**Little Eater Tel.0585-822750** A661 > Worksop, Double back @ roundabout, 200yds on L. Commercial Cafe, Open 7-15-3.30 Mon-Fri. Sat 7-1. Full breakfasts.
Service Area	S	TEXACO / LITTLE CHEF	**Welcome Break, Woodall Services. Tel.01742-486434** Follow the signs off the motorway Granary self service restaurant, shop, phones, games, and toilets. Little Chef. McDonalds, Shell & Texaco fuels, water & air.
Take away	31		**Todwick Fish Bar. Tel.01097-71776** A57 > Worksop, 1st R. 0.5m on R. FISH & CHIPS Open 11.30-2 &6-10 (Thurs -Fri 5.30-12) Closed Sun.
Cafe Diner	31		**The Roadside Cafe Tel.0860-968947** A57 > Sheffield, 0.5m in layby on R. Open 7.30am-3pm Mon-Fri. Hot & Cold food & drinks, omelettes etc.
REPAIRS	31		**Motor Vehicle Services Tel.01742-879214 Fax.879214** A57. > Sheffield, 1st R, cross road & 1st R. Full garage repairs, 24 hour recovery, service.
Hotel	31		**Red Lion Hotel Tel.01909-771654 Fax.773704** A57 > Worksop, 1.5m on R. (past lights.) *** Hotel Warm welcome,Bar & restaurant, En suite rooms.
Hotel	33		**Swallow Hotel Tel.01709-830630 Fax.830549** > Rotherham, L @ 1st roundabout > West Bawtry Rd. 200yds on R. *** Hotel, 17 mtr pool & Leisure Club, Conference rooms, Restaurant.
Pub Grub	35		**The Sportsman's Tel.01142-468147** A 629 > Rotherham, 0.75m on L. Open 11.30am-11pm. Carvery menu & a la carte.(not Sun)Families welcome.
Take away	35		**Shelley's Fish & Chips Tel.01142-467734 Fax.467734** A629 > Rotherham, 0.75m on R Open 7am-2 &4.30-12pm. Breakfasts, & Fish & Chips.
FUEL	35		**Scholes Service Station. Tel.01742-457124** A629 > Rotheram, 0.5m on L Esso Fuels, Car wash. Lottery, Esso Shop.
Pub Grub / Restaurant	36	BREWERS FAYRE / SPECIAL OFFER	**Wentworth Tel. 01226-350035** A61 > Sheffield, at the junction with the A616. (1 m. Off) Our delicious menu provides a wide selection of value for money meals, as well as our own "daily specials". We look forward to welcoming you. Baby changing facilities.Toddler area. Fun Factory. Garden. Childrens Parties. Outdoor play equipment. Disabled facilities. Accommodation. Breakfasts.

REPAIRS	36	FINA	**Hilltop Service Stn. Tel.01226-284412** A61 > Barnsley 1m on R. Open 6.30-9 (7 days), Full workshop, All Fuels + Key Fuels. Shop,Micro,
Take ~away	36		**Birdwell Fish & Chips Tel.012262-360043** A61 > Barnsley, 0.5m on L Open 11.30-2 &6-12 (7 days). Fish & Chips, Kebabs, Pizzas, Chicken.
Pub Grub	36		**The Cock Inn Tel.01226-742155** A61 > Barnsley, > 1st L 400yds down hill on L. Very traditional pub serving Bar meals, Kids play area, & beer garden.
cAMPINg	36		**Green Springs Touring Park Tel.01226-288298 Fax.288298** A61 > Barnsley 1st L > Pilley, 1 on L Open Apr-Oct. Caravans & tents, Hookup, Showers,Set in woodland.
Hotel	36		**Tankersley Manor Tel. 01226-744700 Fax.745405** A61 > Sheffield, 0.5m on L. *** 17th. Century Hotel, ideal for business or pleasure.
Pub Grub Restaurant	37	BREWERS FAYRE	**Lord Nelson Tel. 01226-762324** SPECIAL OFFER A628 > Penistone, in the village of Hoylandswaine. (3.8m Off) Our delicious menu provides a wide selection of value for money meals, as well as our own "daily specials". We look forward to welcoming you. Baby changing facilities.Toddler area. Garden. Childrens Parties.
Take ~away	37		**Fish & Chips & Kebab** A 628 > Barnsley, 0.75 m on L. Fish & Chips, Open 11.30am -2pm & 5pm-11.30pm.
Pub Grub	37		**The Gate Inn Tel.01226-282705** A628 > Manchester, 400yds on L. Open 12-3 & 6.30-11. Families welcome, Pool table, Bar snack specials,
FUEL	37	Shell	**Shell, Barnsley Tel.01226 737100** A628 > Barnsley, 0.5m on R OPEN 24hrs.Shell Select Shop, microwave snacks, & ice creams. Jet Wash.
Pub Grub Restaurant	38	BREWERS FAYRE	**Black Bull Tel. 01924-830260** SPECIAL OFFER A637 > Flockton, (2m Off) Our delicious menu provides a wide selection of value for money meals, as well as our own "daily specials". We look forward to welcoming you. Baby changing facilities. Garden. Childrens Parties. Disabled facilities.
Relax Cafe Diner	38		**Yorkshire Sculpture Park Tel.01924-830302** A637 > W.Bretton, 0.75m on L. One of Europe's leading open air galleries situated in 100 acres of beautiful 18th century parkland of the former estate of Bretton Hall, with a changing program of exhibitions. Facilities include a cafe, book and craft shop, and free Booster Scooters for those with limited mobility.
Relax	38		**Bretton Country Park Tel.01924 830550** A637 > W.Bretton, 0.25m on L. Country Park with Henry Moore Sculptures. Free Entry, Parking fee.
Cafe Diner	38		**Tea Bar Tel. 0374-949046** A637 > Huddersfield, 100yds in layby on L. Open 9-3, Mon-Fri, Hot & Cold food & drinks. Burgers,Hot Dogs etc.

Pub Grub	38		**The Old Post Office Tel.01226-378619** A637 > Barnsley, on L. Open 11.30-3, & 5-11. Coffee, Bar meals, Beer garden, Kids play area.
Relax	38		**Woolley Edge** Follow the brown signs from the junction. Layby with SUPERB VIEWS.
Service Area	S		**Granada, Woolley Edge Services. Tel.01924-830371** Follow the signs off the motorway. Restaurant, Burger King, shop, phones, Granada Lodge.
Hotel	39		**Cedar Court Hotel Tel.01924-276310 Fax.280221** A636 > Denby Dale, 50yds on L. Hotel, conference specialists, International Restaurant,Cocktail bar.
Relax	39		**Pugneys Country Park Tel.01924-302360** A636 > Wakefield, R at roundabout 20 yds. Windsurfing & sailing. Board & Dinghy hire. Free Parking, Burger van.
Hotel	39		**Hotel Campanile Tel.01924-201054 Fax.201055** A636 > Wakefield, over river & canal, > L on L. Large modern Hotel, Restaurant & Bistro,Good meeting room facilities
SUPER STORE	39		**Asda** A636 > Wakefield, R @ roundabout, around side of lake, 2nd on L. Open 8.30am-10pm. Sat 8-8, Sun 9.30-4.30. All fuels and Jet wash.
Pub Grub	40		**The Commercial Inn Tel.01924-274197** A638 > Ossett. 1st L. 1.5m on L. Open all day, drink & coffee. Home cooked food,(12-2.30 & 5-7.30)
FUEL	40	Shell	**Shell Ossett Tel.01924-261027** A638 > Wakefield, 300yds on L OPEN 24hours. Shell Select Shop, microwave snacks, ice creams, jet wash.
Hotel	40		**Forte Posthouse Tel01924-276388 Fax.276437** A638 > Wakefield, R at the lights, 50 yds on L All the facilities you have come to expect from a smart modern hotel
B&B	41		**The Poplars Tel.01924-375682** A650 > Wakefield, 1st L. > Carrgate 0.5m 0n L. All rooms en suite. Tea, coffee & TV. Full cooked English Breakfast.
FUEL	41	Mobil	**Manor Service Station. Tel.01924-822260** > E. Ardsley, 200yds on L. All Fuels, Shop with microwave snacks.
Pub Grub	41		**The Bay Horse Tel.01924-825926** A650 > Bradfield, 500yds on R. Open all day, Full menu & bar snacks, Tetley Quality Food House.
REPAIRS	43		**Kwik- Fit Tel.01132 700117** A61 > Leeds, L @ lights, through next lights, 0.75m on R. Full range of tyre repairs.
Pub Grub	43		**The Punch Clock Tel.01132774165** A61 > Leeds, L @ lights & L @ 2nd lights, on R. Smart modern pub serving real ale, good food and coffee.
			Please remember to mention "Just Off..." **when you visit one of our locations**

	Exit		
Hotel	43	JET	**Jet Service Station Tel.01132-709842** A61 > Leeds, 100 yds on L. OPEN 24 hours, All Fuels, car wash, Shop with microwave and coffee.
REPAIRS	43		**Goodman Tyre Services. Tel.01332-719770** A61 > Leeds, 200 yds on R. Open 9am-4pm. Tyres & all car repairs.

	Exit		
Take-away	2		**Jade East Tel.01634-724024** > Rochester >L by BP stn. 200yds on L. (1.5m from M-way) Full Chinese menu. Why not phone ahead.
Pub Grub	2		**The White Hart Tel.01634-711857** A228 > Snodland 0.5m. on L. Families welcome, Food 12.30-2.15 & 7-10, Coffee all day.
Take-away	2		**Darnley Rd. Fish Bar. Tel.01634-717286** > Rochester, > L. by BP stn. 210 yds. on L. Fish & Chips, 11.30am -11 pm (Closed Sunday)
Hotel	3		**Forte Posthouse,Rochester. Tel.01634-687111 Fax.684512** A229 > Chatham, 1m on L. Full leisure facilities and all rooms en suite, Restaurant, bars.
cAMPing	3		**Woolmans Wood Camping Park Tel.01634-867685 Fax.670090** A229 > Rochester, > B2097 follow brown signs to park. Open all year, Shower block, hookup, a delightful spot.
Relax	3		**Picnic Area** A229 > Maidstone, follow the brown signs. Car park and picnic area with superb views, watch height restriction.
Pub Grub	4		**The Hungry Fox Tel.01634-387552** > Gillingham, L @ roundabout, R @ end of road & R @ next roundabout. Open all day, Food 12-2.30 & 7-9.30 Speciality Steaks, real ale.
SUPER STORE	4		**J.Sainsbury Plc. Sava Centre Tel.01634-373511** > Gillingham, L @ 1st roundabout, around next, follow signs for petrol. Open 8.30am-8pm. All fuels, Restaurant in Super Store.
Service Area	S	Shell	**Pavilion, Medway Services. Tel.01634-233343** Follow the signs Burger King, Cash (Barclays.) Card machine, Lodge.ESSO, SHELL
FUEL	5	Shell	**Glen Eagles Self Service Stn. Tel.01795-842236** A249 > Sittingbourne, 0.5m on L. OPEN 24 hours, All fuels,Shell Shop with Microwave snacks.
Cafe Diner	5		**Danaway Cafe** A249 > Sittingbourne, 0.75m on R. All day breakfast, Hot & cold food, Daily Specials, sandwiches.
Cafe Diner	5		**The Happy Eater Tel.01795-843277** A249 > Maidstone, 1m on L. (4m back to M-way) Open 7am-10pm. Licensed, Full Happy Eater menu, Kids menu.

REMEMBER – Tiredness kills – TAKE A BREAK

B&B	6	**Preston Lea Tel.01795-535266 Fax.533388** A251 > Faversham, > R. A2 Canterbury, 500 yds on L. ETB** Highly Commended, fine house & gardens, All Rooms ensuite.
cAMPInG	6	**Painters Farm Camp Site. Tel.01795-532995** A251 > Faversham, > L on to A2 Sittingbourne, next L Follow sign. Tents & Vans, Easy reach of coast & Ports, Hook ups and showers etc.
Pub Grub	6	**The Windmill. Tel,01795-536505** A251 > Faversham, R >A2 Canterbury, 200 yds on L. parking @ rear. Pub with full menu & snacks, 4 rooms B&B with drinks & TV.

Cafe Diner	3	**Jack's Tel.01276-473193** A322> Bracknell, L >A30 Camberley. Open 7-11, every day. Full all day breakfast, Fish & Chips from noon.
REPAIRs	3	**Roadwheel Tyre & Exhaust Ltd., Tel.01276-475577 Fax.451968** A322 > Bracknell, L @ lights, R @ Mini roundabout, 500yds on L. Open 8-6 (Sat 8-5) Tyres, Wheels, Exhausts, Brakes, Batteries etc.
FUEL	3	**B.P Service Stn. Tel.01276-472736** A322 > Bracknell, L >A30 Camberley, 600yds on L. Open 24 hrs. Small shop,Microwave snacks, Car wash.
Pub Grub	3	**The White Hart Tel.01276-473640** A322> Bracknell, L @ lights, R @ mini roundabout Open all day for coffee & bar snacks. Meals 12-2.30 & 6-9pm.
Restaurant	4	**The Crab & Dragon Tel.01276-22578** > Farnborough, L @ roundabout, > Frimley. L @ roundabout, L > Camberley on L. Open 11-3 & 5-11 English &Thai food, restaurant & bar.menu, traditional Beer
SUPER STORE Cafe Diner	4	**J.Sainsbury Plc. Tel.01276-676829** A30 > Basingstoke, 0.5m on R. Low price petrol, Car wash, Coffee shop serving hot and cold food. all normal super market goods available in the main store. PETROL Station open 6.30 am - 10 pm. Monday - Saturday, (7.30 - 8 Sunday).
Pub Grub Restaurant	4	**Willems Park Tel. 01252-344063** A321 then A325 > Aldershot. On Wellington r'bout, next to Tesco. Our delicious menu provides a wide selection of value for money meals, as well as our own "daily specials". We look forward to welcoming you. Baby changing facilities.Toddler area. Fun Factory. Garden. Childrens Parties. Outdoor play equipment. Disabled facilities. Accommodation. Breakfasts.
Pub Grub Restaurant	4	**Monkey Puzzle Tel. 01252-546654** > Farnborough, next to Golf Club Our delicious menu provides a wide selection of value for money meals, as well as our own "daily specials". We look forward to welcoming you. Baby changing facilities. Play Zone. Garden. Outdoor play equipment. Disabled facilities.
Take -away	4	**McDonald's Tel.01252-371943** > Farnborough, R @ roundabout, R @ mini roundabout, across next & L >Park. Open 7-12, 7 days /week. Full McDonald's menu with drive through.

Service Area	S	Shell LITTLE CHEF	**Welcome Break, Fleet Services. Tel.01252-621656** Follow the signs off the motorway Granary self service restaurant, shop, phones, games, and toilets. Little Chef and Travel Lodge, baby change and disabled facilities. McDonald's, Shell fuels, water & air.
Pub Grub	5		**The Jolly Miller Tel.01256-702085 Fax.704030** B3349 > Odiham, 1m on L. Camping, B&B, Restaurant, Meeting room, Open all day,Sun12-3 &7-10.30
Take ~away	5		**Roadside Snack Bar Tel.01252-21401** A287 > Farnham, for 2m in Layby. Open 9-4 weekdays., Burgers, Rolls, Drinks etc, tables & chairs.
Restaurant	5		**Blubeckers Mill House Tel.01256-702953** A287 > N.Warnborough, R. @ roundabout > Odiham 200yds on R. Beautiful Mill offering great food & warm hospitality. Kids play area.
SUPER STORE FUEL	6	IIIIIII TESCO	**Tesco Super Store, Basingstoke Tel.01256-840206** Follow A33 > Reading @ 4th roundabout up on R. (2.2m) Petrol Station open 6am-Midnight. Facilities at this Super Store include:- Baby changing toilets.
Pub Grub Restaurant	7	BREWERS FAYRE	**Down Grange Tel. 01256-461149** A30 >Basingstoke, in parkland on L after Kempshot r'bout. Our delicious menu provides a wide selection of value for money meals, as well as our own "daily specials". We look forward to welcoming you. Baby changing facilities.Toddler area. Fun Factory. Garden. Childrens Parties. Outdoor play equipment. Disabled facilities.	SPECIAL OFFER
2	7		**The Queen Inn. Tel.01256-397367 Fax. 01256-397601** > Dummer Village, through village slowly, on R. 15thC.Beautiful surroundings with large fireplace, low beams & resident ghost. Open 7 days/week. This is somewhere special. Fine restaurant & Bar snacks.All food is home made. Our speciality is a steak & kidney pud for those with a hearty appetite. Tables outside in summer. A very, very friendly welcome.	SPECIAL OFFER
Pub Grub Restaurant	10	BREWERS FAYRE	**Percy Hobbs Tel. 01962-849631** A31 > Alresford. (3 miles Off.) Our delicious menu provides a wide selection of value for money meals, as well as our own "daily specials". We look forward to welcoming you. Baby changing facilities.Toddler area. Garden. Childrens Parties. Outdoor play equipment. Disabled facilities.	SPECIAL OFFER
cAMPINg	10		**Morn Hill, Winchester Tel. 01962-869877** Follow A31 > Alresford, > R. Opposite the Percy Hobbs Pub, (3m. Off) Open 31st Mar- 30 Oct (8am-8pm) Caravan Club open to non members.
Pub Grub Restaurant	12	BREWERS FAYRE	**Captain Barnard Tel. 01962-712220** A31 >Winchester, next to Compton Nurseries. (1 m off). Our delicious menu provides a wide selection of value for money meals, as well as our own "daily specials". We look forward to welcoming you. Baby changing facilities. Play Zone. Garden. Children's Parties. Outdoor play equipment. Disabled facilities.	SPECIAL OFFER
			REMEMBER – Tiredness kills – TAKE A BREAK

Service Area	**S**	**Mobil**	**Granada, Heston Services. Tel.01815-747271** Follow the signs off the motorway. Restaurant, Burger King. shop. fax & passport photo booth, Granada Lodge
SUPER STORE **FUEL**	**3**	**IIIIIIII** **TESCO**	**Tesco Super Store, Hayes Tel.01815-693510** A312. Hayes, 0.4m @ roundabout 3rd exit > Hayes Rd. Petrol Station OPEN 24 hours. Facilities at this Super Store include:- Coffee Shop. Non dispensing Pharmacy, Cash dispenser. Baby changing and toilet
Pub Grub	**5**		**The Montague Arms, Tel 01753-543009** A4> Langley,600 yds. on L. Open 11-11, Food 12-2.30 &5.30-10.30. Families welcome, Over 21's Bar.
FUEL	**5**	**Mobil**	**Brands Hill Filling Station. Tel,01783-581522** A4 > Staines, 200yds on L. OPEN 24 Hr. All Fuels, Jet Wash, Shop with Microwave Snacks.
B&B	**6**		**Rainworth Guest House Tel.01753-856749 Fax.859192** A355 > Windsor down to Windsor r'bout, A308 > Maidenhead 2 m L > B3024 on L. A large and spacious private house set in 3 acres of peaceful grounds, Excellent accommodation, traditional comfort & warm hospitality. Tennis court in grounds, Riding, swimming, golf & Squash available locally. Close to Windsor Castle & Great Park. Race Course, River Thames & Eton.
cAMPINg	**6**		**Windsor Touring Caravan Park Tel,01753-851501 Fax.868172** A355 > Windsor, first turn off to Windsor roundabout, A308 > Maidenhead 1m on R Touring Caravan Park, (Opening Spring 1997) Check details before arrival.
Pub Grub	**6**		**Ye Olde Red Lion Tel.01753-863892** A355 > Windsor down to Windsor r'bout, A308 > Maidenhead 2 m then L > B3024 The Red Lion is about 300 yds around the corner, 2nd Pub on the Left. 18th century Pub serving bar food and A La Cart Restaurant with daily specials Large Garden Open 7 days per week, Closed Sunday evenings Opening times 12-2.30 pm & 6-11pm.
Pub Grub	**6**		**The Windsor Lad, Harvester Restaurant Tel.01753-864634** A355 > Windsor, first turn off to Windsor roundabout, A308 > Maidenhead 1m on R Fresh, Tasty & wholesome Food.
SUPER STORE **FUEL**	**6**	**IIIIIIII** **TESCO**	**Tesco Super Store, Slough Tel.01753-516345** A355 > Slough, 0.7m @ lights turn R. > A4. Petrol Station OPEN 24 hours. Facilities at this Super Store include:- Coffee Shop. Dispensing Pharmacy, Baby changing and toilets.
Pub Grub	**6**		**Earl of Cornwall, Tel.01753-578333** A355 > Slough, 1st L by Copthorn. Modern Pub, open all day Food 11-3, Kids welcome @ lunch time.
Hotel	**6**		**Courtyard Hotel, Tel.01753-551551** A355 > Slough, > R @ roundabout. Modern, All rooms en suite with hot drinks,Restaurant (12-2.30, 7-10).
Take -away	**6**		**New Lantern. Tel. 01753-579159** A355> Slough, 1st on L, past Copthorn, on L by Earl of Cornwall. Open Mon-Sat 12-2 & 5-11. Chinese, Preorder for quick service,

M4 Exit

FUEL	**7**	**ESSO**	**Esso Fuel Station** > R at the roundabout, through two lights on R. Full forecourt service
REPAIRS	**7**		**Hi-Q Tyres and Exhausts Tel.01628-663237** > R at the roundabout, on the L at second lights. Tyres and Exhausts fitted Mon -Fri. 8.30-5.30 Sat 8.30-12.30.
Restaurant	**7**		**Tummies Bistro Tel.01628-668486** > R at the roundabout L @ second lights on the L behind Hi-Q tyres. A lively Bistro with good menu Open Mon-Fri 12-3 & 6-12 Sat 6-12.
Take-away	**7**		**Kentucky Fried Chicken** > R at the roundabout, through two lights on R. Usual KFC Menu. Open 11.30- Midnight (Fri & Sat closing 1am.)
Take-away	**7**		**McDonald's Drive Through** > R at the roundabout, through two lights on L. Full Burger bar menu
Pub Grub **Restaurant**	**11**		**The Swan, Tel.01734-883674** A33 > Basingstoke, 1st. L > Three Mile X on L. OPEN ALL DAY, old coaching Inn. Oak beams. Inglenook etc., Businessman's Pub & meeting place, renowned for real ales & freshly home cooked Food. Small lunch time restaurant, hot meals cooked to order all day. Large car park & garden at rear.
Restaurant	**11**	LITTLE CHEF	**Little Chef Tel.o1734-313465** > A33 Reading, 0.75m on R. Open 7am-10pm. Full Little Chef menu all day. Licensed & adjacent to Fuel.
FUEL	**11**	**Shell**	**Shell Fairfield, Tel.01734-312976** A33 > Reading, 600 yds on R. OPEN 24 Hours.Shell Select Shop, Microwave snacks, Car wash & vacuum
Service Area	**S**		**Granada Reading Services** > Follow the signs Separate east & West bound areas Restaurant, shop, Lodge, Card printer, Cash machines Burger King.
Pub Grub **Restaurant**	**12**	BREWERS FAYRE	**Mansion House Tel. 01189 505125** A4 > Reading, 2 m. in Prospect Park, > Liebenrood Rd, on L. Our delicious menu provides a wide selection of value for money meals, as well as our own "daily specials". We look forward to welcoming you. Baby changing facilities. Garden. Childrens Parties. Disabled facilities.
REPAIRS	**12**		**Rapid Fit Tel.01734-453323** A4 > Reading 0.7m on L. Open 8.30-6 (Sun 10-4) Tyres, Exhausts, Clutches Brakes,Service,MOT.
Restaurant	**12**		**Gathering Tel.01734-303478** A4 > Newbury R @ 1st junction>Theale, in High St. on R. Restaurant / Pub, Brasserie & snacks. Parking @ rear.
FUEL	**12**	**BP**	**Polygon Retailing Ltd. Tel.01734-421266** A 4 > Reading, 0.8m. on L. Open 7am -11pm., Small shop, air & water,All Fuels.
SUPER STORE	**12**		**J.Sainsbury Plc. Tel.01734-416451** A4 > Reading, L @ roundabout. Open 24hr for FUEL., Cafe in store, open 8.30am-7pm.

	Exit		
Service Area	13		**Granada, Newbury Services. Tel.01635-248024** Follow signs from roundabout. Restaurant, Burger King, shop, phones.
Pub Grub	13		**Ye Olde Red Lion, Tel.01635-248379** A34 > Oxford. 1st. > Chievely, 500yds.on L. Food 12-2.30 & 6.30-9.30. Kids welcome, Real Ales, Log fires, B&B,
Pub Grub	14		**The Pheasant Inn, Tel.01488-648284** A338 > Oxford, 1st. L. >Lambourn. 200yds on L. Fine Views, Food & Bar snacks 12-2.15 & 6.30-9.30. Families welcome.
B&B	14		**Fishers Farm Tel.01488-648466 Fax.648706** A338 > Wantage, 1st L > B4000 Lambourn, 800 yds.On R. Open All year.,All rooms en suite,& Hot drinks, Swimming pool,
REPAIRS	14		**Great Shefford Auto Centre, Tel.01488-648055 Fax.648760** A338 > Wantage, through village, 2m. on R. Open 8.30-5.30 (Sun 9.30-12.30) Repairs,& Tyres Exhaust.etc.
Service Area	S	BP / LITTLE CHEF	**Welcome Break, Membury Services. Tel.01488-71881** Follow the signs off the motorway Granary self service restaurant, Little Chef, baby change and disabled facilities. shop, phones, games, and toilets. B.P. & Shell fuels, water & air.
Pub Grub	15		**The Plough Inn, Tel.01793-740342** A346 > Marlborough, 400yds up hill on R. 17th C. Inn..Full Menu served 11-2 & 6 30-9-45. Garden & play area.
FUEL	15		**Chiseldon Camp Service Stn., Tel.01793-740251** A346 > Marlborough, over hill on the R. OPEN 24 hours every day. ESSO petrol and diesel. Snack and Shop, BAKERY, Car Wash, All Credit Cards accepted.
Hotel	15		**Forte Posthouse, Tel.01793-524601 Fax.512887** >Cirencester >A4259 Swindon @ roundabout 3rd exit. *** Hotel, Leisure facilities, 98 rooms, Food all day.
Take-away	16		**Wroughton Fish Bar, Tel. 01793-812426** B4005 > Wroughton, 1st L. 2m. > R. on R. Open Mon-Sat 11.45-1.30 &5-10. (Sun 5.30-10) JUMBO COD ! Parking,
Hotel	16		**Hilton National Tel.01793-880777 Fax.881881** A3102 > Swindon, 100yds.on L. ****Hotel, 24 hour (night porter) Swimming pool & leisure facilities.
Cafe Diner	17		**Hideaway Truck Stop. Tel.01249-750645** > RAF Lyneham, .5miles on R Key Fuels & Diesel Direct. Park up, Cafe, showers etc.
Pub Grub Restaurant	17	BREWERS FAYRE	**Cepen Park Tel. 01249-462096** A350 > Chippenham, R @ r'bout, on R opposite Safeways. Our delicious menu provides a wide selection of value for money meals, as well as our own 'daily specials'. We look forward to welcoming you. Baby changing facilities.Toddler area. Play Zone. Garden. Childrens Parties. Outdoor play equipment. Disabled facilities.

Pub Grub	17		**The Plough, Tel.01249-750255** A 350 > Chippenham, 1.5m. on R. @ lights. Built in 1650, Open 11-3 & 6-11.Full menu, Kids welcome. Good parking.
Hotel	17		**The Bell House Hotel, Tel.01249-720401 Fax.720401** > Sutton Benger, Hotel in the centre of village, on R.. RAC ***, Tourist Board 4 crown, Egon Ronay Recommended.
SUPER STORE	17		**Safeways Super Store, Tel.01249-657922** A350 > Chippenham, R @ roundabout, L @ next roundabout. All Fuels, Car Wash, Cafe in store.Open 7am-10pm (Sun 8-8)
FUEL	17	MURCO	**Murco Service Stn., Tel.01666-837161** A 429 > Cirencester, 0.5m. on L OPEN 24 hr. All fuels, Gas, Jet Wash, & shop.
Pub Grub	17		**Radnor Arms, Tel.01666-823389** A429 > Malmsbury, in Corston on L. on the bend.! (3 m Off) Warm Welcome, very Good food, Good beer, open 7 days a week.
Service Area	S	ESSO	**Granada, Leigh Delamere Services. Tel.01666-837691** Cash (Barclays, Link & NatWest.) Burger King,Shop A.J's Restaurant, Restaurant, Burger King, AJ's Family Restaurant, games, shop, Granada Lodge.
B&B	18		**Chestnut Farm, B&B. Tel.01454-218563** A46 >Acton Turville, >1st. R, 0.5m on L. 3 twins, 2 Double, en suite with TV.
Relax	18		**Picnic Area.** A46. > Bath. 100yds > R. Quiet Picnic area, with signed walks, part of the Cotswold Way.
Pub Grub	18		**The Crown, Tel.01225-891231** A46> Bath, on L at the cross roads. Generous Home cooking, keen priced, B&B, real ale, play area.
Hotel	18		**The Compass Inn, Tel.01454-218242 Fax.218741** A46 > Old Sodbury, 300yds. turn R. 150 yds on R. High Class fine old inn, Conference rooms, Restaurant open 7 - 9.30pm
Service Area	21	ESSO	**Pavilion, Severn View Service. Tel.01454-632851** Signed from motorway. Esso Shell, Pavilion Lodge, Shop Restaurant, Cafe, Card Machine.
Pub Grub / Restaurant	22	BREWERS FAYRE	**Piercefield Tel. 01291-622614** A466 > Monmouth, 2 miles N of Chepstow in village of St Arvans. Our delicious menu provides a wide selection of value for money meals, as well as our own "daily specials". We look forward to welcoming you. Baby changing facilities. Garden. Play Zone. Children's Parties. Outdoor play equipment.
Hotel	22		**The Old Course Hotel. Tel.01291-626261 Fax.626263** A466 > Chepstow, R @ roundabout 200 yds on L. All rooms en suite, TV, trouser press. 24 hour reception.
Pub Grub	22		**New Inn, Tel.01291-622670** A466 L @ roundabout 0.5 m. down hill on L. Bar snacks, open fires, fine 200yr. old pub, Open 11-11 Food 12-9.30.
			Please remember to mention "Just Off..." **when you visit one of our locations**

	Exit		Details
Service Area	23	ESSO	**Granada, Magor Services. Tel.01633-880111** Travel Lodge,(O800 555300) Burger King, Granada Restaurant, Esso fuel, Restaurant, Burger King. shop. fax & passport photo booth, Granada Lodge
Pub Grub Restaurant	28		**Stonehouse Tel. 01633 810541** A48 > east. @ r'bout > Newport Docks, R into Lighthouse Rd. Pub is on L. Our delicious menu provides a wide selection of value for money meals, as well as our own "daily specials". We look forward to welcoming you. Baby changing facilities.Toddler area. Garden. Children's Parties. Outdoor play equipment. Disabled facilities.
REPAIRS	28	ATS.	**ATS. Tyres & Exhausts Tel.01633-216115** Follow signs to town centre, through roundabout, over bridge & L. 0.5m on L. Open 8.30am. -5.30pm. (12.30 on Sat) Just Tyres.
Pub Grub Restaurant	32		**Radyr Arms Tel. 01222-843185** A470 > Merthyr, .5 m. turn L > B4262, In Radyr > L into Station Rd. (2.8m Off) Our delicious menu provides a wide selection of value for money meals, as well as our own "daily specials". We look forward to welcoming you. Baby changing facilities.Toddler area. Garden. Childrens Parties. Outdoor play equipment. Disabled facilities.
Hotel	32		**Mason Arms Toby Hotel, Tel.01222-692554 Fax.693724** A470 > Cardiff, 1.5 m. on L. (@ third set of lights.) Attractive modern Hotel 24 hour service all rooms TV,en suite,T.press
Take-away	32		**McDonald's Tel.01222-691700 Fax. 626413** > Super Store on L. Fast food Burgers Shakes hot & cold drinks.
FUEL	32	BP	**Whitehead Motors, Tel.01222-610513** A470 > Cardiff,1.5m. on L (3 sets of lights.) OPEN 24 hours.All Fuels, Shop.
FUEL	32		**ASDA Stores Ltd. Tel.01222-613213 Fax.521844** Follow the signs for super store. Open for fuel 24 hr,Car wash,large shop, Lottery, & Super store.
Service Area	33	ESSO	**Pavilion, Cardiff Services. Tel.01222-891141** Follow signs. Lodge, Shop, Restaurant, Cafe, Barclay cash machine, Information desk.
FUEL	34	JET	**Jet Corner Park, Tel.01443-224115** A 4119 > Rhondda, 1.5m. on L. All fuels, Small Shop.
Restaurant	34		**The Barn at Mwyndy Tel.01443-222333** A4119 1.5 m on R Opposite Jet Petrol Stn. Open 11.30-2.30 & 5.30-11. Over 21's Restaurant,Stylish Barn by lake,
Relax	34		**Llanerch Vineyard, Tel.01443-225877 Fax.225546** Signposted from the junction, just 1m south. The largest vineyard in Wales, producing estate bottled wines. Visitor centre and coffee shop for refreshments.Vineyard tours with winetastings Ample free parking Woodland walks for picnics. 1995 Welsh Tourism Award Winner. Children's play area. Open March to December 10am-5pm every day.
Pub Grub	35		**Old Kings Head Tel.01656-860203** A473 > Pencoed. L @ roundabout, next R; 200yds. on R. Rolls & sandwiches all day, Beer Garden, Kids welcome, Open 11am- 11pm

	Exit		
Pub Grub Restaurant	35	BREWERS FAYRE	**Pantruthyn Farm Tel. 01656 860133** Take exit by Gulf garage, Pub is immediately on R. Our delicious menu provides a wide selection of value for money meals, as well as our own "daily specials". We look forward to welcoming you. Baby changing facilities. Fun Factory. Garden. Childrens Parties. Outdoor play equipment. Disabled facilities. Accommodation. Breakfasts. *(SPECIAL OFFER)*
Take-away	35		**Coasters Tel.01656-766616** By Jet Service Stn. on roundabout. Open 9-5. All day breakfasts, Hot dogs, Hot & Cold Drinks.
SUPER STORE **FUEL**	35	‖‖‖‖‖‖ TESCO	**Tesco Super Store, Bridgend Tel.01656-647117** A473 > Bridgend. (3m off) Petrol Station OPEN 24 hours. Facilities at this Super Store include:- Coffee Shop. Dispensing Pharmacy, Home & Wear. Cash dispenser. Baby changing and toilets.
REPAIRS	36		**Autofix. Ltd. Tel.01656-766033 Fax.668041** In the service area 24 hour brakedown service. RAC agent. Full assistance.
Service Area	36	Shell LITTLE CHEF	**Welcome Break, Sarn Park Services. Tel.01656-655332** Follow the signs off the motorway Granary self service restaurant, shop, phones, games, and toilet Little Chef and Travel Lodge, baby change and disabled facilities. Tourist information centre. Microwave snacks at the fuel station. Shell fuels, water & air.
Hotel	36		**Mason's Arms Hotel. Tel.01656-720253 Fax.724538** A4061 > Bryncethin, 0.5m on R. Smart private hotel, all rooms en suite TV,Hot Drinks etc.,Good Food
SUPER STORE	36		**J.Sainsbury Plc. Tel.01656-648951** > Bridgend, Super store on R. 24hr. Fuel, car wash, small shop. CAFE in store
REPAIRS	36		**Tyres R Us. Tel.01656-720044** A4061 > Bryncethin. Open 9-5.30 (Sat 9-1) Full Tyre repair service, including balancing,
REPAIRS	37		**Central Garage, Tel.01656-740322** A48 > Pyle, once in Pyle it's 200yds on L. Fuel (open 8-7) Repairs, Tyres, Exhausts, (Workshops 9-5.30)
Cafe Diner	37		**Snack Bar, Tel.01656-742413** A48 > Pyle, L @ roundabout > N.Cornelly on L. @ junction. Open 8am-5pm. All day breakfast, Pies & Pasties
FUEL	37	BP	**Porthcawl Rd. Service Stn., Tel.01656-740039** A4429 > Porth Cawl, L @ roundabout,> S Cornelly, on L. All Fuels, Shop with microwave snacks, Toilets.
Cafe Diner	38		**The Abbot's Kitchen, Tel.01639-891548 Fax.872179** A48 > Pyle, 1st on L. Open 10-5. Breakfast till 11.30, Sunday lunches speciality.Good walks
Hotel	38		**The Twelve Knights, Tel.01639-882381** A48 > Port Talbot, on L. (1.5 m.) Accommodation and bar food etc.,

M4	Exit	*Margam Country Park (E of Exit 38), Iron Age Fort, 12th Century monastery and museum*

Pub Grub	**38**	**Lakeside Country Inn Tel.01639-883496** A48 > Pyle 2nd R. then on R.(approx1.5m from motorway) Open 11-11. all day food, bar snacks & restaurant, Golf course.
Take-away	**41**	**Mair's Fish & Chip Bar, Tel.01639-820005** A474 > Briton Ferry, on L down the hill. FISH & CHIPS. Open 11.30-2.30 & 6-11 (Closed Sun.)
Take-away	**42**	**Baglan Bakeries, Tel.01639-813010** A48 >Baglan, 500yds on R. Savouries, filled rolls, Hot potatoes, Hot & Cold drinks.
Take-away	**43**	**McDonald's** A465 > Neath, 100 yds on L. Open 24 hours.
SUPER STORE FUEL	**44**	**Tesco Super Store, Swansea East Tel.01792-702121** A48 > Swansea East 1mile turn L. A4217. Petrol Station OPEN 24 hours. Facilities at this Super Store include:- Coffee Shop Baby changing and toilets.
FUEL	**44**	**D.F.A.M.Bevan Tel.01792-8175405** A4230 > Skewen 500yds on L. Open 24hrs. All fuels air & water.
Pub Grub	**44**	**Ye Olde Plough & Harrow Tel.01792-700344** A48 > Swansea, R @ 2nd lights, 200yds on L. Open 11am-3 & 5.30-11pm. Full menu & bar snacks
Take-away	**44**	**Golden Palace, Tel.01792-776409** A48 > Abertawe, 500yds down hill on R. Wide selection of Chinese Food, Why not phone your order ahead..
CAMPING	**45**	**Riverside Caravan Park Tel.01792-775587** Follow the signs off the roundabout under the motorway. Open all year, Heated indoor pool, Hook up, Laundry, Club house.
Pub Grub	**45**	**The Old Glais Tel.01792-843316** A4067 > Pontardawe, R @ roundabout over bridge on R. Open 7 day /week food 12-2 &7-11, Kids welcome,restaurant & bar food.
REPAIRS	**45**	**Free Fit Services Tel.01792-792774** > Morriston Hospital, on L opposite Police station. Tyres & exhausts. Open 8.30-5.30 Sat 8.30-4.
SUPER STORE FUEL	**47**	**Tesco Super Store, Swansea West Tel.01792-587738** A483 > Swansea Petrol Station OPEN 24 hours. Facilities at this Super Store include:- Coffee Shop Baby changing and toilets.
Pub Grub	**47**	**The Old Inn** A48 > Penllergaer, on L at mini roundabout Clean friendly pub food served 12-2.30 & 6-11
Take-away	**47**	**Ray's Snack Bar Tel.01792-894900** A48> Morriston, 400yds in layby on R All day breakfasts, Rolls Hot drinks, Open 8am-3.30pm.

Service Area	47	TEXACO	**Pavilion, Swansea Services, Tel.01792-894894** 24hr services Texaco Fuel & cash machines, Accommodation, Restaurant, Snack bar, Shops Barclays Bank Cash point,
Pub Grub	48		**Smith's Arms Tel.01554-8203053** A4148 > Llanelli 1st L 400 yds on L. Open all day (Food 12-3pm) Coffee all day, Families very welcome.
Take away	48		**Hendy Fish Bar** A4138 > Hendy 0.5 m up hill on L. Fish & Chips Open 12-1.30 & 6-11.
Pub Grub	48		**The Black Horse Inn Tel.01792-882239** A4138 > Hendy 0.5m on L. Open all day Restaurant, food served 12-2.30 & 6.30-9.30.
Service Area	49	BP	**Road Chef, Pont Abraham Services. Tel.01792-884663** BP, Restaurant, Tourist information, Natural gift shop, Barclays cash dispenser, Games Toilets.etc.,

Service Area	S	BP	**Granada, Frankley Services. Tel.01215-503131** Follow the signs Restaurant, Burger King, shop, phones, Granada Lodge.
Hotel	1		**Bearwood Court Hotel Tel. 01214-299731 Fax, 296175** > A4252, L @ 2nd r'bout L onto A457 then filter R immediately after lights into High St. R @ one way system, R @ lights (Bearwood Rd), hotel on R. (2.5m Off) ** AA Hotel, 24 bedrooms, most en suite. Bed & Breakfast. Evening meals 7pm - 8.30pm. Illuminated and secured car park. Conference rooms. This is a very friendly, good value, family run hotel.
Pub Grub Restaurant	2	BREWERS FAYRE	**Lakeside Tel. 01215-523031** A4123 > Wolverhampton, through 1st lights 600yds on L. Our delicious menu provides a wide selection of value for money meals, as well as our own "daily specials". We look forward to welcoming you. Baby changing facilities.Toddler area. Fun Factory. Garden. Childrens Parties. Outdoor play equipment. Disabled facilities. Accommodaton. Breakfasts.
B&B	4		**Home Farm B&B Tel.01527 874964** A491 > Stourbridge, 1st L , then 2nd R. Straight forward Bed & Breakfast in farm house. Ground floor accommodation
Pub Grub	4		**Wildmoor Oak, (The Inn on the Stream). Tel.01214-532696** >A491 Stourbridge, 2nd L> Top Rd., 200yds on L. (1m Off) Traditional Pub Home made dishes. Varied menu, from snacks to large steaks, Fish and Vegetarian menu Ample car parking and Beer Garden.
Pub Grub Restaurant	5	BREWERS FAYRE	**Ewe & Lamb Tel. 01527-871929** A38 > Bromsgrove 4m, turn R >B4091 300 yds on R (3.2 m Off) Our delicious menu provides a wide selection of value for money meals, as well as our own "daily specials". We look forward to welcoming you. Baby changing facilities. Play Zone. Garden. Childrens Parties. Outdoor play equipment.

Cafe Diner	5		**Sunnyside Cafe, Tel.01527-861374** A38 > Bromsgrove, 50 yds. on L. OPEN 7am-5pm Mon-Fri. Large Transport Cafe, Cheap Eats, Good Grub,
Pub Grub	5		**The Robin Hood, Tel.01527-861224** A38.Droitwich, 400yds on L. Ian and Deborah invite you to their traditional roadside Inn. Offering Real Food, Real Ale, and a Real Welcome. A wide range of home cooked food available. Children are welcome. Safe and secure garden with play equipment. Drop in and see us and you will always return.
Restaurant	5	LITTLE CHEF	**Little Chef & Travel Lodge Tel.01527-861594** A38 > Droitwich, 800yds on R. Open 7am-10pm, Licensed. baby change & disabled facilities. Travel Lodge. Fuel.
Pub Grub	6		**The Poachers Pocket, Tel.01905-458615 Fax.458840** > Warndon, 0.5m on R. Full menu & Vegi, Pub hours Food 12-2 &6-10.Meeting room, V.Friendly.
Take -away	6		**Chreg Catering (Mobile) Tel.01905-45161** A449 > Kidderminster, Layby on L. OPEN 8am-4pm. Burgers, Hot Dog, Sandwiches & Drinks.
Pub Grub	6		**The Bull Inn, Tel.01905-451509** A449 > Kidderminster, 1st turning L, R > A4539 Fernhill Heath .2m @ junction. Open all day, food until 6pm, Bar snacks until 9pm. Kids Welcome.
SUPER STORE	6		**J.Sainsbury Plc.** A449 > Kidderminster, 1st L, L again, A4539 > Blackpool, L @ roundabout. No Diesel, No Cafe, Just Petrol & Super Store.
Pub Grub	6		**Speed the Plough, Tel.01905-345602** >Evesham, 1m. L @ roundabout, 1m. Lunchtime & evening food (except Thurs lunch). Good home cooking.
FUEL	7	BP	**Rottner & Rudge Ltd., Tel.01905-351245** A44>Worcester, cross 1st roundabout, cross 2nd roundabout around 3rd. on L. All Fuels, Jet wash, small shop.
Relax	7		**The Countryside Centre, Tel.01905-766493** A44> Worcester, cross roundabout, R @ next roundabout follow signs. CAFE, 50 acres to ramble,Kids Swings, Open 10-5 all year.Guided walks.
Pub Grub	7		**The Swan, Tel.01905-35361** A44 > Worcester R on roundabout. Open 11-3 & 5-11 (Food 12-2 & 6.15-9.30). This pub has a unique style. There is something different about the Swan, and it's very pleasing, the decor is unusual yet very relaxing. The food is excellent, home cooking with a varied menu. There is good parking, a large garden with tables and a childrens' play area.
Service Area	S	BP	**Take a Break Services, S. Bound ONLY. Tel.01684-293004** Follow the signs off the motorway. Jet Burger. Restaurant. Patisserie. Shop. Lottery. Cash Point. B.P.
Service Area	S	TEXACO	**Take a Break Services, N. Bound ONLY. Tel.01684-293004** Follow the signs off the motorway. Jet Burger. Restaurant. Patisserie. Shop. Caravan Stop. Lodge. Lottery. Texaco.
B&B	9		**Spa-villa Guest House, Tel.01684-292487** A438 > Tewkesbury. on L. (0.5m.) Large Guest House, Open all year, H & C, TV, Hot drinks. Car Park.

	Exit		
B&B	9		**Newton Farm, Tel,01684-285903** A438 > Stow on R. (0.3m). All rooms en suite,TV,Hot drinks. Pleasant Farm House. open 24 hours.
FUEL	9	BP	**B.P. Fuel Services.** A438 > Stow 350 yds on R. All fuels, Large shop.
SUPER STORE	9		**Safeway Tel.01684-273268** A438 > Tewkesbury,on R. (0.8m) Open7-9. (Fri.7-10,Sun7-5) Fuel, Cafe & Carwash,
Restaurant	9	LITTLE CHEF	**Little Chef Tel.01684-292037** A438 > Stow, 400yds on R. Open 7am-10pm, Full menu, Licensed. Adjacent fuel.
Hotel	11		**Golden Valley Thistle Hotel. Tel.01242-232691 Fax.221846** > Cheltenham on the L. @ next roundabout. Modern****Hotel,Open 24 hrs,All rooms ensuite,satellite TV.etc.Leisure.
cAMPINg	11		**Stansby Caravan Park, Tel.01452-712168** A40 >Cheltenham,>R @ next roundabout.follow signs (2 m.) Tents & Vans, showers, hookup, Calor & Gaz, Dogs permitted. open all yr
Pub Grub	11		**The Pheasant Inn, Tel.01452-713246** A40> Cheltenham, 1st L @ roundabout, >Staverton on R. Country Pub open all day, for food and drink.
SUPER STORE FUEL	12	TESCO Southbound Only	**Tesco Super Store, Quedgeley Tel.0Tel.01452-0720717** B4008 > Gloucester, @ roundabout > A 38, then L. into Bristol Rd. Petrol Station open 7am. - midnight. Facilities at this Super Store include:- Coffee Shop, Dispensing Pharmacy, Baby changing and toilets
Pub Grub	13		**The George Inn Tel.01453 890270** A419 > Dursley, A 38 > Bristol. 3miles on the R. (3m Off) Food & Coffee all day. Childrens corner. Large car park. SPECIAL OFFER
cAMPINg	13		**The George Inn Caravan and Camping Tel.01453 890270** A419 > Dursley, A 38 > Bristol. 3miles on the R. (3m Off) Riverside camp site, beside good pub with food. Hook ups, showers etc.
FUEL Restaurant	13	Shell LITTLE CHEF	**Oldbury Services Tel.01453-828688** A419 > Stroud, @ 1st roundabout on L. OPEN 24 HOUR, Petrol. & Diesel, Large shop & microwave refreshments. Air line and water available. Car wash. Adjacent to Little Chef.
FUEL	13	JET	**Fromebridge Garage, Tel.01452-740753** >A419 Dursley, L @ roundabout, >A38 300yds on L. Open 7am-7pm. All types of fuel.
Hotel	13		**Whitminster Hotel, Tel.01452.740234 Fax.741403** >A419 Dursley, >A38 Gloucester, 1m. on R. Bar Meals. Evening Restaurant. Function room & en suite bedrooms.
Pub Grub	13		**The Old Forge, Tel.01452-741306** >A419 Dursley, > R. A38 Gloucester, 1m. on R. All Day food & coffee, open fires. kids welcome. Lounge bar.

B&B	13		**Kings Head, Tel.01453-822934** A41 > Stroud R @ roundabout, 1m. to centre of village. Good Food, Families welcome, Beer Garden,Trad. Ales.
Service Area	**S**	**Mobil**	**Welcome Break Service Area.** Large gift shop, Granary Restaurant, Julies Pantry, Business card machines, Phones, Mobil Fuels.
Hotel	14		**The Park Hotel, Tel.01454-260550** >B4509 Falfield, turn L >A38 1m. on L. A private hotel in very pleasant surroundings,All rooms en suite & TV.
FUEL	14	**Mobil**	**Mill Lane Filling Station, Tel.01454-260286 Fax.261583** B4509 > Falfield R > A38, 300yds on R. Open 7.30-10.30 (24 hour breakdown), Repairs, Car wash, all fuels.
Pub Grub	14		**The Huntsman, Tel.01454-260239** >B4509 Falfield, turn L > A38, 200yds on R. Bar snacks, Full menu, pleasant atmosphere, Draught beer. No children,
Hotel	14		**The Gables Inn, Tel.01454-260502 Fax.261821** > B4509 Falfield, turn R. >A38 200yds on R. Smart, modern, all rooms en suite,restaurant, Gym, Conference room etc
Pub Grub **Restaurant**	16		**Masons Arms Tel. 01454-412370** A38 > Gloucester 3 miles on R. Our delicious menu provides a wide selection of value for money meals, as well as our own "daily specials". We look forward to welcoming you. Baby changing facilities.Toddler area. Garden. Childrens Parties. Outdoor play equipment. Disabled facilities.
SUPER STORE **FUEL**	16	**TESCO**	**Tesco Super Store, Bradley Stoke Tel.01454-618578** A38 > Filton, 0.3m @ 1st exit, Bradley Stoke over next r'bout, R @ next r'bout. Petrol Station open 6am. - midnight. Facilities at this Super Store include:- Coffee Shop. Baby changing and toilets.
B&B	16		**The Jays Guest House, Tel.01454-612771 Fax.898333** A38.>Bristol, through Aztec roundabout, 100yds on R. En suite rooms with hot drinks & TV,Excellent English breakfast.
Take ~away	17		**McDonald's Drive Through** Follow the signs to the Hypermarket on the L. Full Burger bar menu
REPAIRS	17		**Kwick Fit** Follow the signs to the Hypermarket, between Asda & McDonalds. Tyres and Exhausts fitted Mon -Fri. 8.30-5.30 Sat 8.30-12.30.
Service Area	17		**Asda** Follow the signs to the Hypermarket Fuel and full shopping facilities.
Pub Grub	17		**The Fox, Tel.01454-632220 Fax.632220** >B4055 Easter Compton, Down the hill, 1m. on L. Open 11am-2.30pm & 6pm-11pm.,Sundays 12.am- 3pm. & 7pm-10.30pm.
Restaurant	17		**The Lamb & Flag Harvester. Tel.01179-510490** > A4018 follow signs for Zoo, on R. Open for Breakfast from 7 am, Lunches 11-2.30, Evening Meals 5-10.30.

Restaurant	**17**		**Harry Ramsden's Tel.01179-594100 Fax.500233** A4018 > Cliffton, L @ roundabout, 50 yds > R. Open for Fish & Chips. Eat in or Take-away, Sun-Thur 11.30-10.30, Sat 11.30-11.
Hotel	**17**		**Travel Lodge Tel.0800-8305** > A4018 Follow signs for Zoo, on R. Open 7am-10pm. All rooms en suite, TV, Tea & Coffee etc.
Service Area	**19**	**Shell** LITTLE CHEF	**Welcome Break, Gordano Tel.01275-373624** Follow the signs off the motorway Granary self service restaurant, Little Chef and Travel Lodge, baby change and disabled facilities. shop, phones, games, and toilets. Shell fuels, water & air. Tourist Information Centre.
Pub Grub	**19**		**The Rudgleigh Inn, Tel.01275-372363** > A369 Clifton, on L. (0.6m.) Open all day, Food 12-2.30 & 7-9.30. Kids Welcome, No Coaches.
SUPER STORE **FUEL**	**20**	‖‖‖‖‖‖ TESCO	**Tesco Super store, Clevedon Tel.01275-340567** B3133 > Clevedon, 1st exit @ roundabout, 3rd exit @ next roundabout. Petrol Station open 7 am-12 pm. Facilities at this Super Store include:- Coffee Shop. Dispensing Pharmacy, Cash dispenser. Baby changing and toilets.
B&B	**20**		**Moorvillas B&B. Tel.01275-872131** > B3133 cross roundabout, 300 yds on L. Open all year. All bedrooms have TV, basins,& hot drinks
REPAIRS	**20**		**Winter Stoke Tyres, Tel.01275-342473** > B3133 Clevedon, Cross roundabout, > L @ next roundabout, on R. Open 8.30-6 pm (Sun 9-1) Tyres, Exhausts, Batteries, Brakes. (Coffee)
Pub Grub *Restaurant*	**21**	BREWERS FAYRE SPECIAL OFFER	**Old Manor Tel. 01934-515143** > Weston, R > Sand Bay @ 1st junction. cont. to Sand Bay over 3 r'bouts, on R Our delicious menu provides a wide selection of value for money meals, as well as our own "daily specials". We look forward to welcoming you. Baby changing facilities. Toddler area. Fun Factory. Garden. Childrens Parties. Outdoor play equipment. Disabled facilities.
Pub Grub	**21**		**The Summer House, Tel.01934-520011** >A 370 > L @ roundabout, on the L. Open 11-2.30, 5.30-11, Coffee. Pub lunches. Restaurant. Kids Welcome.
FUEL	**21**	BP	**Weston Motoring Centre, Tel.01934-511414** > A370, > R @ roundabout on L. All Fuels, small shop, friendly staff.
Pub Grub	**21**		**The Woolpack Inn. Tel.01934-521670** > A370 Weston-Super-Mare, > 1st R., 200 yds on L. Large Garden for Kids. Restaurant. Bar Food 12-2.30,& 6-11. Log Fire,
Service Area	**S**	**Shell**	**Welcome Break, Sedgemoor, N. Bound ONLY. Tel.01934-750730** Follow the signs off the motorway Granary self service restaurant, and La Baguette fast brake take-away. shop, phones, Games, Card Machine. Travel Lodge for over night accommodation. Shell fuels, water & air.

Service Area	S	**ESSO**	**Road Chef, Sedgemoor Services. S. Bound ONLY. Tel.01934-750730** Follow the signs off the motorway. Road Chef restaurant and shop. Tourist information.
B&B	22		**Priors Mead Tel.01278-782116** > Burnham, R @ r'about into Love Lane, >3 L off Stoddens Rd.(2.9 m.off) Edwardian home with pool/gardens. Ensuite.TV, drinks etc.,
Cafe Diner	22		**The Goat House, Tel.01278-760995** > A370 Weston-Super-Mare, 0.5m. on R. Open 8am-5pm. Family Restaurant. Visit the Goats & buy their produce.
cAMPINg	22		**Home Farm Holidays Park, Tel.01278-792365 Fax.788888f** > Burnham on Sea, on the R. Tents, caravans & campers. Showers & Club House.
Relax	22		**Combes's Cider, Tel.01278-641265** >A38 Bristol, > 1st R. >R @ cross rd. (2.5m from Motorway.) Cider Farm & Museum. Tea rooms. Summer Opening 9-5.30 (Sun 12-2.30)
cAMPINg	22		**Edithmead leisure & Park Homes, Tel.01278-783475** > A38 Highbridge, > L @ roundabout, on L. Tents & Vans, showers. Licensed Club. Entertainment. Take-away.
Hotel	22		**Battleborough Grange Hotel, Tel.01278-760208 Fax.760208** A38 > Bristol one mile on L. RAC **, Les Routier. Michelin.
Hotel	22		**Royal Clarence Hotel Tel.01278-783138** B 3140 > Burnham, follow the road to the sea front. 200yds on R. The Royal Clarence Hotel is an old coaching Inn, with well appointed bedrooms.
Take-away	23		**The Frying Scotsman, Tel.0850-7034732 (mobile)** >A 39 Glastonbury, over hill, L. in lay bye.(0.75m.) Mobile, Open 7am-3pmish. Sandwiches. Burgers etc & much more.
Pub Grub	23		**Puriton Inn, Tel.01278-683464** >A 39, Glastonbury, 200 yds on the L. Draught beers. Children very welcome. Morning Coffee. Conference room
B&B	23		**Rockfield House, Tel.01278-683561** Just off motorway, > A39 Glastonbury, 0.5 m. on R. All rooms H&C, TV,Tea & Coffee facilities. Evening meals. Car Parking.
Pub Grub Restaurant	24		**Quantock Gateway Tel. 01278-423593** > Bridgwater, A39 > Minehead, 1 m. out of Bridgwater. Our delicious menu provides a wide selection of value for money meals, as well as our own "daily specials". We look forward to welcoming you. Baby changing facilities. Play Zone. Garden. Childrens Parties. Outdoor play equipment. Disabled facilities.
FUEL	24	**Mobil**	**Westside Motors Tel.01278-427486** >A38 Bridgewater, cross next roundabout, 200yds on R. All fuels, small shop, car wash,
B&B	24		**Quantock View Guest House, Tel.01278-663309 Fax.663309** >A38, Taunton, L. @ roundabout 250yds on L. Open till 10pm.TV, Showers, Coffee machines in all rooms,advise booking.
REPAIRS	24		**National Tyre & Autocare Tel.01278-422745** A38 > Bridgewater, cross the roundabout, 0.5 m. on R. 1 hour Tyre & Exhaust service, Open 8.30 am-5.30 pm Mon - Sat.

Pub Grub	24		**Boat & Anchor Inn. Tel.01278-662473** > Huntworth, keep L. & over the canal bridge. Canalside Inn, Bar meals, restaurant, B&B, function room, play area.
Pub Grub Restaurant	25	BREWERY FAYRE	**Bathpool Tel. 01823-272545** > Taunton, .5mile, A38 > North. .5 mile on R.(1mile Off.) Our delicious menu provides a wide selection of value for money meals, as well as our own "daily specials". We look forward to welcoming you. Baby changing facilities. Play Zone. Garden. Childrens Parties. Outdoor play equipment. Disabled facilities.
FUEL	25	**MURCO**	**Murco Service Station** Just off the roundabout Full range of fuels and shop.
B&B	25		**B&B at Barn Close Nurseries, Tel.01823-443507** A358,>Yeovil,past cross rd. beside Post Office on L. Family welcome, Drinks & TV in rooms, Full Breakfast, pool in summer.
SUPER STORE	25		**J.Sainsbury** > A358 Taunton, R @ roundabout on the R. Open 7am-8pm,Sun 8.30am-8pm.,All Fuels. Car wash.
cAMPIng	25		**Ashe Farm Caravan & Camping Site, Tel.01823-442567 Fax.443372** >A358 Yeovil, 2.5m. on R @ Nag's Head. Tents & Tourers, Lovely surroundings,showers, hot water. Tennis court.
Restaurant	25		**Pizza Hut. Tel.01823-444747** >A358 Taunton, R @ roundabout follow Road to Texas. Open 12am-11pm, Fri & Sat.12-12. Licensed, range of Pizzas & salads.
Pub Grub	25		**Blackbrook Tavern, Tel.01823-443121** >A 358 Yeovil 200yds on L. Open for drinks and coffee all day, lunches 12am-2pm. Children welcome
Service Area	S	BP	**Road Chef,Taunton Dean Services. Tel.01823-271111** Follow the signs off the motorway, Restaurant on both sides, Card machine,Games, Shop.
FUEL	26		**Piccadilly Service Station, Tel.01823-662148** >A38 Taunton R @ Roundabout >A38 Taunton 400yds. on L. Discount. Fuels. Independent Trader, shop.
Pub Grub	26		**The Blackbird Inn, Tel.01823-461273** >A38 Taunton, R @ roundabout >A38 Taunton, lm. on L.(Parking on R.) Open 11-3 & 6-11. Bar Snacks. Kids welcome, B&B. Meeting room. Garden.
Relax	26		**Willowbrook Garden Centre, Tel.01823-461324** >A38 Taunton, @ roundabout >A38 Taunton, 1m on R. Open 9-6 Wide range of plants & Cafe offering home cooked food.
FUEL	27	**ESSO**	**Kellands Garage, Tel.01884-820264** >A361 Tiverton,1st L. > Sampford Peverell, on R. All Fuels and an extensive shop.
FUEL	27	Shell	**Shell Tiverton Tel.01884-821353** >A 38 Wellington, 100yds. on R. OPEN 24 hrs. Shell Select Shop, microwave snacks, oils, Little Chef adjacent.
Restaurant	27	LITTLE CHEF	**Little Chef, Tel.01884-821205** >A38 Wellington, 100yds on R. Open 7am-7pm. All day Breakfast, Coffee Stop.

Icon	Exit	Logo	Details
Hotel	27		**Parkway House Hotel. Tel.01884-820255 Fax.820780** A361 > Tiverton, 1st L > Sampford Peverell, on R. Meeting/conference rooms. Bedrooms en suite, AA rosette restaurant.
cAMPINg	27		**Minnows Caravan Park Tel.01884-821770** >A361 Tiverton, L @ 1st Juncton follow the signs. Tents and Caravans welcome, small site with showers. Closed February.
Pub Grub	27		**Globe Inn, Tel.01884-821214** >A361 Tiverton, 1st L > Sampford Peverell, in middle of village. Open all day,2 bars, good range of snacks. Children welcome, garden,
Relax	27		**A convenient Lay bye, with view.** >A38, Tiverton, 100yds on L. Offering views of open fields.
Hotel	27		**Travel Lodge, Tel.01884-821087** >A38 Wellington, 100yds on the R. Usual high standard of Travel Lodge facilities. All rooms en suite & TV.
REPAIRS	28		**Continental Cars Specialists Tel. 01884-34124** > Cullompton, just after police station > into Forge way, 50 yds on R. Open 8.30 am - 5.30 pm Monday to Friday . General workshop facilities , sales service & parts supplied Call out and breakdown service.
B&B	28		**Court Cottage Tel.01884-32510** >A373 Cullompton, 0.5 m. on R opposite the Police Station. Charming, 3 bedrooms with TV.,2 bathrooms, 3 mins. from the High St.
Pub Grub	28		**The Weary Traveller, Tel.01884-32317** >A373>Cullompton, over bridge on L. Normal pub hours, Bar meals. Happy hour 5-6pm. Children's play area.
Hotel	28		**Manor House Hotel, Tel.01884-32281** >A373 Cullompton turn L into main street on R. High class Hotel open all day for refreshment. Rooms en suite with TV.
FUEL	28	JET	**CCS FORD Tel.01884-33795 Fax.38479** >A373 Cullompton, on the L. Open 6am-10.30pm. Shop, phone, car wash, quick fit & repair centre.
Take away	28		**Fish & Chips Tel.01884-32667** >A373 Cullompton, Turn R into main street, on L opposite car park. Chinese & Fish & Chips. Open 12am-2pm &5.30-11 pm.(Closed Tuesdays).
Service Area	S	ESSO	**Granada, Exeter Services. Tel.01392-436266** Follow the signs from the motorway. Restaurant, Burger King, photo booth, card machine, games, shop, Granada Hotel.
Pub Grub	30		**The Blue Ball Inn, Tel.01392-873401** >A3052 Sidmouth, all the way round the roundabout > Exeter, > 1st L.on R Coffee all day, Food 12-2.30 & 6.30- 9pm (7 day a week).
SUPER STORE FUEL	30	TESCO	**Tesco Super Store, Exeter Tel.01392-445425** A379 > Exeter/Dawlish 1st L > Superstore Petrol Station open 6am. - midnight. Facilities at this Super Store include:- Coffee Shop. Non dispensing Pharmacy, Home & Wear. Cash dispenser. Baby changing and toilet. Harry Ramsdens Restaurant. Travel Lodge.

Pub Grub	**30**	**The Half Moon Inn, Tel,01392-873515** >A3052 Sidmouth, L @ roundabout > village centre, on L. Morning Coffee. Lunches, & Evening Meals, B&B. friendly & clean..
REPAIRS	**30**	**Rydon Motors, Tel.01392-877922** >A3052 across roundabout > Sidmouth, 200yds on L. Repairs, Tyres, full garage facilities, friendly service.
Pub Grub	**31**	**Gissons Hotel Tel. 01392-832444** Continue towards Plymouth > 2nd L > Kenford Services (2.2m Off) Good Food (Carvery etc.). Accommodation, Large Car Park (Height restriction 8.5ft

Pub Grub	**1**		**The Haywaggon Tel.01788 8323207** A426 > Lutterworth, 1st L > Churchover, in the village. Country pub, Italian Chef, English & Italian food. 11-2 & 7-10 (not Sun Eve).
B&B	**1**		**North Field House Farm Tel.01455-554507, x Mobile 0850-031398** A426 > Lutterworth, across roundabout 1st farm on L. B & B. All rooms with TV, basins, coffee and tea.
FUEL _Service Area_	**1**	TEXACO	**Gibbets Cross Service Station Tel 01788-860747** A426 > Lutterworth, R @ roundabout. OPEN 24 hours. 365 day a year. Hot drinks. Sandwiches. Hot food. Newspapers. Confectionery. Ice creams. Groceries. Calor Gas. Payphones, disabled toilets and nappy changing facilities.
SUPER STORE	**2**		**ASDA** A4600 > Coventry Central & North, Through roundabout on L. Fuel, Coffee shop, Pharmacy, Photo booth. Open 8.30-8 (Sun 10-4)
Hotel	**3**		**Novotel, Coventry** B4113 > Bedworth, R @ roundabout 50yds. on L. Modern hotel, en suite rooms. Conference facilities.
FUEL	**3**	JET	**Cornwall Motoring Centre Tel.01203-362698** A444 > Nuneaton, 1st L. & L. @ bottom of hill, 0.25m on L. Open 7-9 Mon-Sat, 8-9 Sun. All Fuels, low prices. Tyres, exhausts, batteries.
Service Area	**S**	Shell / LITTLE CHEF	**Welcome Break, Corley Services. Tel.01676-40111** Follow the signs off the motorway Granary self service restaurant, Little Chef with disabled facilities. shop, phones, games, and toilets. Shell fuels, water & air.
Service Area	**S**	Shell	**Pavilion, Hilton Park Service. Tel.01922-412237** Follow the signs off the motorway. Shell & Esso, Restaurant 7 Lodge.
Pub Grub	**11**		**The Wheatsheaf Tel.01922-412304** A460 Cannock, 400 yds on L. Open all day, drinks & coffee, food served 12-2 & 6-8,30. Steaks a speciality.
Pub Grub	**11**		**The Elms Tel.01922-412063** A460 Wolverhampton, 0.75m > R. 400yds in village. Fine ales. Home cooked food. Good menu. Kids welcome.

Hotel	11	**Featherstone Farm Hotel & King's Repose Restaurant, Tel.01902-725371** A460> Wolverhampton. >R @ lights, on R. A small high class hotel in 5 acres of unspoilt countrysise. 8 bedrooms, all en-suite and usual facilities. Self-contained cottages with service available. The King's Repose Restaurant is a meticulously converted medieval barn and we are very proud of our top class menus. Secure parking.
FUEL	11	**Shareshill Service Station Tel.01922-415378** A460 > Wolverhampton, 0.75m on R. Open 7.30-7.30, All fuels, shop.
REPAIRS	11	**Shareshill Garage Tel.01922-410757** A460 > Wolverhampton, 0.75 m on R. Open 8am-5.30pm. Full garage workshop, MOT's, repairs, servicing.
FUEL	11	**Gatley Service Station Tel.01902-791172** A5 > Telford 0.75m on R. Open 6.30am-10pm. All fuels, Jet wash, shop with microwave snacks.
Pub Grub	12	**Milestone Restaurant, (Spread eagle). Tel.01902-790212** A5 > Telford, 1m across roundabout on R. Open 11-3 & 5-11, Sat.all day. Families welcome, Real Ale & good food.
Cafe Diner	12	**Hollies Transport Cafe Tel.01543-503435** A5 > Cannock, 0.5m on L. OPEN 24 hrs. A nice clean and tidy cafe with full menu.
Hotel	12	**Oak Farm Hotel Tel.01543-462045 Fax.462045** A5 > Cannock, 1 mile on L. Cosy, picturesque hotel, en-suite rooms, conference facilities, ETB 3 Crown.
Hotel	13	**The Garth Hotel Tel.01785-56124 Fax.55152** A449 > Stafford, 1m on R. Fine bedrooms en suite, Carvery restaurant, and light snack pantry in the bar.
FUEL	13	**Mosspit Garage Ltd. Tel.01785-54428** A449 > Stafford, 0.5m on L. Open 7am-9.30pm. All fuels & shop.Full workshops, repairs & servicing (8.30-5.)
Hotel	14	**De Vere Tillington Hall Hotel. Tel.01785-53531 Fax.59223** A5013 > Stafford, on L. Friendly & relaxing hotel, leisure club with indoor pool, conference rooms.
FUEL	14	Shell **Great Bridgeford Garage Tel.01785-282221** A5013 > Eccleshall. 1.5m on L. Open 7.30-8. All fuels & small shop.
Pub Grub Restaurant	15	**Poachers Cottage Tel. 01782-657115** A500 > Stoke take slip Rd to A34 > Stone on R next to Trentham Gdns. (2.4m Off). Our delicious menu provides a wide selection of value for money meals, as well as our own "daily specials". We look forward to welcoming you. Baby changing facilities.Toddler area. Garden. Childrens Parties. Outdoor play equipment. Disabled facilities.
B&B	15	**Trentside Private Hotel Tel. 01782-642443 Fax.641910** A500 > Stoke , 1st slip Rd A34 >Stone. On R (U turn next @ r'bout) (2.3m Off) B & B in comfort, Tea / Coffee, Colour TV. Off Rd. parking.
Hotel	15	**Forte Posthouse Tel.01782-717171** A519 > Newcastle-U-Lyme, 200 yds on L. Modern in 5 acres, Restaurant, all day bar, leisure facilities & meeting rooms.

FUEL	15	BP	**Swift Service Station Tel.01782-713308** A519 > Newcastle,-U-Lime, 0.5m on R. Open 7am-10pm. All fuels, garage workshop.
Take~away	15		**P. & C. Catering Tel.01783-680622** A500 > Stoke 500 yds in large layby on L. Mobile open 7.15 am- 4pm. Mon -Fri. for food and drink, hot or cold.
SUPER STORE **FUEL**	15	||||||| TESCO	**Tesco Super Store, Stoke Tel.01782-636914** A500 > Stoke, 1.3m L.> Newcastle & then 1st exit @ roundabout > A34. Petrol Station open 6am. - midnight. Facilities at this Super Store include:- Home and Wear. Baby changing and toilets.
Service Area	S	Shell / LITTLE CHEF	**Welcome Break, Keele Services. Tel.01782-626221** Follow the signs off the motorway Granary self service restaurant, shop, phones, games, and toilets. Little Chef with disabled facilities. K.F.C. Cash point Shell, Texaco, Total fuels, water & air.
Take~away	16		**Jim's Snacks. Tel.01782 305115** A500 > Chester 300 yds. in Layby on L. Mobile serving hot & cold food and drinks.
Restaurant	16	LITTLE CHEF	**Little Chef & Travel Lodge Tel.01270-883115** > Radway Green, 200 yds. on L. Open 7am-10pm. Licensed. baby change & disabled facilities. Travel Lodge. Fuel.
FUEL Service Area	16		**Barthomley Service Station Tel.01270-883212** > Radway Green, 200 yds on L. Open 7am-11pm. Excellent service, room for parking, Travel lodge and Little Chef on same site. Emergency Garage services available on request. Discount Fuel Prices.
Pub Grub	16		**The White Lion Tel.0127-882242** > Radway Green, 0.75m > 1st L. into village, on corner. Open all day (Thurs 5.30-11) Bar snacks & coffee. Very traditional.
Service Area	S	BP	**Road Chef, Sandbach Services. Tel.01270-767134** Follow the signs off the motorway. Wimpey, shop,toilets, phones, Shell.
FUEL	17	TEXACO	**Saxon Cross Service Station Tel.01270-765014** A534 Sandbach, 100 yds. on L. OPEN 24 hrs. Large shop with microwave, sandwiches and coffee, Car wash disabled toilets facilities.
Hotel	17		**Saxon Cross Hotel Tel.01270-763281 Fax.768723** A534 > Congleton, 1st L. A5022> Holmes Chapel 300yds on L. Modern *** Hotel. conference centre fine food & comfortable en-suite rooms.
Hotel	17		**Chimney House Hotel Tel.01270-764141 Fax.768916** A534 > Congleton, 0.5m. on R. Situated in secluded countryside, a beautiful tudor style *** hotel in 8 acres.

M6 Exit *Jodrell Bank Radio Telescope, open to public (east of Exit 18)*

Pub Grub | **18** | | **The Fox & Hounds Inn Tel.01606-832303**
> Middlewich, 0.5m on L.
Bar & restaurant meals, parties welcome.

Hotel | **18** | | **The Holly Lodge Hotel Tel. 01477-537033 Fax.535823**
A535 > Holmes Chaple, R at r'bout A50 > Stike on Trent, On R. (1.3 m.)
*** Hotel with 34 bedrooms, restaurant open to non residents, conference rooms.

FUEL | **18** | **SAVE** | **Sproston Auto Point Tel.01606-832387**
> Middlewich. 1m on R.
Open 7am-10pm daily, All fuels and microwave in the shop.

Service Area | **S** | **Shell** | **Pavilion, Knutsford Service. Tel.01565-634965**
Follow the signs off the motorway.
Burger King, Restaurant, Shell.

Restaurant | **19** | | **Little Chef & Travel Lodge Tel.01565-755049**
A556 > Manchester Airport, 200 yds on L.
Open 7am-10pm. Licensed, baby change & disabled facilities. Travel Lodge. Fuel.

Hotel | **19** | | **The Old Vicarage,Private Hotel Tel.01565-652221**
A556 > Manchester Airport. 0.5m on R.
Private hotel with airport parking, all rooms en suite, 3 crown ETB, Licensed

Pub Grub / Restaurant | **20** | | **Crown Inn Tel. 01925-752485**
B5158 >Lymm, 3 miles, L @ T junc. 20 yds on L. (2 m Off)
Our delicious menu provides a wide selection of value for money meals,
as well as our own "daily specials". We look forward to welcoming you.
Baby changing facilities. Garden. Childrens Parties.
Outdoor play equipment. Disabled facilities.

Service Area | **20** | | **Poplar 2000 HGV Services**
Barber shop, News agent, Truckers shop, Cafe, Bar, Mcdonalds drive in. Showers .

Take away | **21** | | **Sheila's Kitchen Tel.01925-755015**
> Birchwood, L @ roundabout.
Mobile Open 8am-2.30pm. Hot & cold food,Baked potatoes, Chillies,Pies.

Hotel | **21** | | **Holiday Inn, Garden Court. Tel.01925-831158 Fax.838859**
B 5210 > Birchwood, 50 yds on L
100 superb bedrooms, meeting rooms, restaurant and bar.

Pub Grub / Restaurant | **23** | | **Miners Lamp Tel. 01744-613040**
> Haydock Park Racecourse, 1st L >Haydock, (2 m Off)
Our delicious menu provides a wide selection of value for money meals,
as well as our own "daily specials". We look forward to welcoming you.
Baby changing facilities.Toddler area. Garden. Childrens Parties.
Outdoor play equipment.

FUEL | **23** | **Shell** | **Haydock Island Service Station Tel.01925-224241**
On the junction roundabout,
OPEN 24 hrs. All fuels, air, water etc.

Restaurant | **23** | | **Little Chef & Travel Lodge Tel.01942-272048**
> Haydock, 1m on L.
Open 7am-10pm. Licensed, baby change & disabled facilities. Travel Lodge. Fuel.

Hotel | **23** | | **Forte Posthouse Tel.01942-717878 Fax.718419**
> Haydock Park, 500 yds on R.
Modern in 10 acres with Fitness club. Pool. Restaurant & bars,

Pub Grub Restaurant	26		**Vale Royal Hotel Tel. 01942-223700** >B5206, L at lights, R @ next lights, Pub is 1 m on R. Our delicious menu provides a wide selection of value for money meals, as well as our own daily specials'. We look forward to welcoming you. Baby changing facilities. Play Zone. Garden. Childrens Parties. Outdoor play equipment. Disabled facilities. SPECIAL OFFER
Pub Grub	27		**The Charnley Arms Tel.01257-424619** A49 > Standish, 0.5m on the R. Fine large pub with outside play area. Food & coffee Mid day -10pm.
FUEL	27	**TOTAL**	**Black Horse Service Station** > Standish 0.5m on R. Open 6am-11pm. All fuels, air, water.
Pub Grub Restaurant	27		**Wiggin Tree Tel. 01257-462318** A5209 > Parbold, on R. (2.5 m Off) Our delicious menu provides a wide selection of value for money meals, as well as our own "daily specials". We look forward to welcoming you. Baby changing facilities. Disabled facilities. SPECIAL OFFER
FUEL	27	BP	**Crow Orchard Service Station Tel.01257-423983** A49 > Ormskirk, on R. OPEN 24 hrs, All fuels, microwave snacks. Jet wash & Vac.
cAMPINg	27		**Gathurst Hall Farm Tel.01257-253464** A49 >Shevington, through the village 2m towards Wigan. Canal side site. Camping. Caravans & campers.
Service Area	S	Shell	**Welcome Break, Charnock Richard Services. Tel.01257-791494** Follow the signs off the motorway Granary self service restaurant, shop, phones, games, and toilets. Little Chef and Travel Lodge, baby change and disabled facilities. La Baguette Shell fuels, water & air.
Hotel	28		**Jarvis Leyland Hotel. Tel.01772-422922 622282** From the slip road under the motorway take the 2nd L > Leyland on L. Fine **** Hotel, restaurant, Lounge bar and business facilities.
Relax	28		**The British Commercial Vehicle Museum Tel.01772-451011** > Leyland Follow the brown signs. Full of fascinating commercial vehicles, well exhibited, Entrance fee.
Pub Grub	28		**The Heyrick Tel;01772-434668** > Blackburn on R @ lights. Open all day, for food drinks & coffee. with family room.
Take -away	28		**The Happy Frier Tel.01772-454949** > Blackburrn, across lights 1st R. Fish & Chips and much, much more. Mon-Sat 11.30-1.30 Eve 4.30-9.
Relax	28		**Car Park & Country Walks** > Blackburn, through the lights, approx 1m on L at bottom of hill Free car park in the country, quiet and away from the motorway.
Pub Grub	29		**The Poachers & Lodge Inn Tel.01772-234100** A6 > Preston, Through the lights next R. on the L. Open for food all day, Funky Forrest, Disabled facilities, informal.

Hotel	**29**		**Novotel, Preston Tel.01772-313331 627868** A6 > Chorley, 1st L. & L again. Modern Hotel with pool, meeting rooms. Sky TV,disabled facilities etc.
SUPER STORE	**29**		**J.Sainsbury Plc.** A6 > Preston, Through lights and take next R. Open for fuel 6am-10pm (7 days) Coffee shop in main store.
FUEL	**31**	**Mobil**	**Riverside Service Station Tel;01772-877656** On the roundabout turn in @ the sign for services. All fuels. Car wash. Jet wash. Coffee microsnacks & phone.
Hotel	**31**		**Swallow Hotel. Tel.01772-877351 Fax.877424** A59 > Blackburn, & junction with A677. *** Hotel with Leisure club & pool, Restaurant & lounge bar.
Hotel	**31**		**The Tickled Trout Tel.01772-877671 Fax.877463** Follow signs to services / Hotel on the roundabout 4 crown ETB,*** hotel. on the banks of the river Ribble.
Hotel	**32**		**Preston Marriott Hotel Tel.01772-864087 Fax.861728** A6 > Garstang, 0.5m on R. ****Hotel, in very fine gardens,leisure club. AA 2 rosette Restaurant
Pub Grub	**32**		**Golden Ball Tel.01772-862746** A6 > Garstang, 1m on L @ lights. Open 11-3 &6-11, All Day Sat & Sun..Traditional Food house & Real ale.
FUEL	**32**	**ESSO**	**Broughton Service Stn. Tel.01772-863604** A6 > Garstang, 1m. on R. at lights. Open 7am-10pm 7days / week, Shop all fuels and microwave snacks.
Service Area	**S**	**ESSO**	**Pavilion, Forton Services. Tel.01524-791775** Follow signs of motorway Burger King, Self service restaurant, Shop Esso
Pub Grub	**33**		**The Bay Horse Inn Tel.01524-791204** A6 > Garstang, > 2nd L. 0.5m on R. Open 11-3 & 6.30-11, Bar snacks & full menu, Trad. English Pub,
Hotel	**33**		**Hampson House Hotel Tel.01524-751158 Fax.751159** A6 > Garstang, 1st L. on L. 4 crown ETB, ** Private Hotel, with conference facilities
B&B	**33**		**Salt Oke South B&B. Tel.01524-752313** A6 > Garstang, > 2nd L. 50 ydson R. Stone house, rural setting, 2 rooms, TV, drinks, h&c Full breakfast, no smoking.
Relax Cafe Diner	**33**		**Canalside Craft Centre Tel.01524-752223** A6 > Lancaster on L. 0.75m Converted stone farm building on banks of Lancaster Canal. Open 10am-5.30pm Tues-Sun. Coffee, home made cakes and meals served all day. Disabled access award winner with large seating area inside and out. Good easy local walks with superb canalside views.
Relax	**33**		**Wyreside Lakes Fishery Tel.01524-792093** A6 > Garstang 1st L follow the brown signs for 2.5m. Open 9-5.Coarse & Game fishing.Tuition. Rod hire. Cafe, Nature trails.
B&B	**34**		**Croskells Farm B&B Tel.01524-65624 Fax. 65624** N. Bound, A683 > K. Lonsdale, / S.Bound A683 > Lancaster. Open all year.Farm B&B. No Smoking.3 rooms with TV & Hot drinks,Pets.

Hotel	34		**Forte Posthouse, Lancaster. Tel.01524-65999 Fax.841265** A683 > Lancaster, On R 100yds. Full Fitness club. Bar. Lounge. Restaurant. Indoor pool.
Pub Grub	34		**The Ship Inn Tel.01524-770265** A683 > Kirkby Lonsdale, in Caton Village on R. (2m from motorway) Home cooked food lunchtime & evenings 7 day. Families welcome, Garden.
Hotel	34		**Scarthwaite Country House Hotel. Tel.01524-770267 Fax,770711** A683 > Kirkby Lonsdale, 1.5m on the R. **Hotel, ETB 4 Crown, Licensed restaurant, Bar Meals, Business facilities
cAMPIng	34		**New Parkside Farm Tel.01524-770723 / 770337** A683 > Kirkby Lonsdale, 1m on R. Tents, Caravans & Campers. Showers & toilets.(Disabled) Hook ups.
cAMPIng	35		**Hawthorn's Caravan Park Tel. 01524-732079 Fax.732079** Follow signs at the T junction on B6254. Tents & Caravans welcome. Hook ups,Showers. Holiday homes for sale.
Service Area	S	**Mobil**	**Granada, Burton Services. N.Bound ONLY Tel.01524-781234** Follow the signs off the motorway. Restaurant, shop, phones,
cAMPIng	36		**Waters Edge Caravan Park Tel. 01539-567708** A65 > Kirkby Lonsdale @ r'bout > Crooklands, 1 m on R. (1m. Off) Set in delightful countryside with easy access to Lake and Peak Districts. Offering a luxury shower block, pool room, licensed bar, TV room, shop, and level hard-standings with electric hook-up. Please ring for colour brochure.
cAMPIng	36		**Millness Hill Country Park Tel.01539-567306** A65 > Kirkby Lonsdale, @ roundabout > Crooklands 100 metres on L. Picturesque award winning park. Caravans, campers & tents, hook-ups, showers.
REPAIRs	36	**Shell**	**J.Atkinson & Son Ltd Tel.01539-567401** A65 > Kirkby Lonsdale, L @ roundabout > Crooklands 1m on R. OPEN 24 hrs. HGV lane, Garage workshop Repairs & servicing.
Hotel	36		**Crooklands Hotel Tel.01539-567432 Fax.567525** A65 > K.Lonsdale, @ roundabout > Crooklands, 1.5 m on R. Delightful Country Hotel with carvery restaurant.and two bars.
Service Area	S	**BP**	**Road Chef, Killington Lake Services. S.Bound ONLY. Tel.01539-620739** Follow the signs off the motorway. Road Chef restaurant and shop, Lodge, BP.
Relax	37		**Parking with fine views** A6847 > Sedburgh. 0.5m. on L. A small peaceful layby ideal for picnics.
REPAIRs	38		**Tebay Car & Commercials Tel.01539-624545 Fax.01539-624584** @ the roundabout > B6260 Old Tebay, on R. Village garage undertaking servicing & repairs to cars & commercial vehicles.
B&B	38		**Primrose Cottage Tel.01539-624791** A685 > Kendal, R @ roundabout, 1st house on R. (0.25m. Off). Evening dinner by arrangement. Range of rooms all with TV. Excellent stop-over or centre for the lakes, Yorkshire Dales. Lovely accommodation, jacuzzi bath, 4-poster bed. One acre garden suitable pets. Very friendly, rural location, also self-contained ground floor flat available.

Service Area	38	Shell	**Westmorland, Junction 38 Services, Tel015396-24505** Follow the signs off the motorway. Restaurant, Shop, toilets, SHELL.
Pub Grub **B&B**	38		**The Cross Keys Inn, Tel.015396-24240** A685, R @ roundabout > Tebay, 0.25 m on R. 400 yr. old coaching Inn.Open for lunchtime bar snacks. There is also a separate restaurant open evenings & weekends. Sunday lunch specials. B&B available in comfortably furnished rooms (TV & H&C). Beware of our friendly ghost Mary Baines said to be the last witch burnt at the stake. Coaches welcome.
Service Area	S	BP	**Westmorland, Tebay Services Tel.015396-24511** Follow Signs Mountain Lodge Hotel. Tebay Caravan Park. Games. Shop. BP
Restaurant	40	LITTLE CHEF	**Little Chef & Travel Lodge Tel.01768-68303** >A66 on L. 0.25 M Open 7am-10pm. Licensed, baby change & disabled facilities. Travel Lodge. Fuel.
cAMPiNg	40		**Waterside House Farm Camp site. Tel.01768-486332** 6 miles from the motorway and worth every inch of the way. A66 > Keswick, @ roundabout > A592 Ullswater, L > Pooley Bridge, through village and then R. Past other camp sites, On the right. Genuine LAKE SIDE and beautiful. Excellent shower and toilet facilities.
Take-away	40		**Eamont Caterers Tel.01768-863345** A66 > Keswick, Double back @ roundabout, 200yds on L in Layby Mobile, Open 8 am-4 pm, Mon-Fri. Hot & cold food etc.
Hotel	40		**Brantwood Country House Hotel Tel.01768-862748 Fax. 890164** A66 > Keswick, L @ roundabout > Ullswater, R >Sainton (3m from motorway) ** Hotel under family management, Very beautiful & friendly.
Relax	40		**Dalemain House Tel.01768-486450 Fax.86223** A66 > Keswick @ roundabout > Ullswater 2m on R. Open 11.15am-5pm. Apr-Oct. Medieval,Tudor & Georgian House, Licen'd restaurant.
cAMPiNg	41		**Thacka Lea Caravan Site Tel. 01768-863319** A6 > Penrith, R at Grey Bull Hotel, down lane on R. (3m Off Spotless showers etc. Town centre 10 mins walk. 2 pubs within 250 yds.
FUEL	41	TEXACO	**Texaco Service Stn. Tel.01768-864019** B5305 > Wigton, 400yds on R. Open 8.30am-6 .00pm Mon - Fri (Sat & Sun 9-1) Fuel & Repairs.
Relax	41		**Hutton in the Forrest** B5305 > Wigton 2.75 m. Open 1pm-4pm,Thur-Sat.Fine middle ages Manor house, cafe and gardens,
cAMPiNg	41		**Woodlands Garage Tel.01768-864019** B 5305 > Wigton, 400yds on R. Open all year. Showers, hard standing, hookup.
Service Area	S	ESSO	**Granada, Southwaite Services. Tel.01697-473476** Follow the signs off the motorway. Restaurant, Burger King, shop, phones, Tourist Information, Granada Lodge.
			Please remember to mention "Just Off..." when you visit one of our locations

	Exit		
Pub Grub **Restaurant**	42		**White Quey Tel. 01228-710577** > Dalston, at Durdar turn L. 1m on L. (2.5 m Off) Our delicious menu provides a wide selection of value for money meals, as well as our own "daily specials". We look forward to welcoming you. Baby changing facilities. Toddler area. Garden. Childrens Parties. Outdoor play equipment. Disabled facilities. *SPECIAL OFFER*
FUEL	42	Shell	**Golden Fleece Service Stn. Tel.01228-42766** A6 > Penrith on L. OPEN 24 hrs.(Closed 4pm -10am Sun) HGV Fuel, microwave & coffee. Cafe at rear.
Cafe Diner	42		**Thistle Cafe** A6 > Penrith on L. Open 7.30am-7pm (Sat.7-12). Transport Cafe behind Shell fuel Station.
Hotel	42		**The Carrow House Tel.01228-32073 Fax. 810334** > Carlisle, R. 200yds. Restaurant & Bar open to non residents, Ideal for business or pleasure
Relax	42		**Small Picnic Area** > Dalston 500 yds on the L. Easy parking.
SUPER STORE **FUEL**	43	TESCO	**Tesco Super Store, Carlisle Tel.01228-595572** A69 >Carlisle 400 yds on R @ lights Petrol Station open 6am - Midnight. Facilities at this Super Store include:- Coffee Shop. Dispensing Pharmacy, Home & Wear, Cash dispenser. Baby changing and toilets.
REPAIRS	43	ATS.	**A.T.S. Tel. 01228-25277** A46 > Carlisle. 1st L. into industrial estate.. Full range of tyres, exhaust and shock absorber services.
B&B	43		**The Warren Guest House Tel.01228-33663** > Carlisle, through 2 sets of lights, on L. opposite Esso petrol stn. 6 rooms en suite with phones, hairdryers & TV, Full English breakfast. Car park.
Pub Grub	43		**The Waterloo** > Hadrians Wall,> Hexham Hot & cold food served at lunch time and evenings.
FUEL	43	ESSO	**Brunton Park Service Station Tel.01228-28715** A69 > Carlisle, 0.5m on L after lights. Open 6am - Midnight. 7 days / week. Car wash. Shop with microsnacks.
Hotel	44		**Forte Posthouse, Carlisle. Tel.01452-613311 Fax.43127** A7 > Carlisle, R @ lights & 1st R. Modern Hotel convenient for business or pleasure. Leisure centre & pool
			Please remember to mention "Just Off..." **when you visit one of our locations**

Pub Grub / Restaurant	**3**	BREWERS FAYRE	**Brucefield Farm Tel. 01506-417788** A899 > Livingston, for 1.5m L onto A71 > West Calder. 1.5m on 2nd r'bout. Our delicious menu provides a wide selection of value for money meals, as well as our own "daily specials". We look forward to welcoming you. Baby changing facilities. Toddler area. Garden. Children's Parties. Outdoor play equipment. Disabled facilities. *SPECIAL OFFER*
cAMPIng	**4**		**Mosshall Farm, Tel.01501-762318** A801, > Blackburn, L @ junction, 0.5m on R Smart site open all year. Caravans, campers & tents. Showers & hookup.
FUEL	**4**	JET	**Mosshall Service Station** A705 > Blackburn, L @ junction, 1m on R. OPEN 24 hours. Jet wash. HGV Fuel. Gas, Cash point. Car wash.
Hotel	**4**		**The Hilcroft Hotel Tel.01501-740818 Fax.744013** A705 > Blackburn, R @ Junction > Whitburn 1m on L. Modern 30 bedroom smart hotel. Ideal for business or pleasure. *SPECIAL OFFER*
Service Area	**S**	BP	**Road Chef, Harthill Services. Tel.01501-517991** Follow the signs off the motorway Restaurant. Shop. B.P.
FUEL	**6**	Shell	**Circular Filling Station Tel.01698-860236** A73 >Lanark, on roundabout. Open 7 days per week 6 am -7.30 pm.
Pub Grub / Restaurant	**6**	BREWERS FAYRE	**New House Hotel Tel. 01698-860277** A73 > Lanark. R @ r'bout..5m on left. Our delicious menu provides a wide selection of value for money meals, as well as our own "daily specials". We look forward to welcoming you. Baby changing facilities. Toddler area. Garden. Childrens Parties. Outdoor play equipment. Disabled facilities. Accommodation. Breakfasts. *SPECIAL OFFER*
Pub Grub / Restaurant	**8**	BREWERS FAYRE	**Springcroft Tel. 01417-733494** A8 > Glasgow through junction (Safeways) .3 m on L. Our delicious menu provides a wide selection of value for money meals, as well as our own "daily specials". We look forward to welcoming you. Baby changing facilities. Toddler area. Outdoor play equipment. Childrens Parties. *SPECIAL OFFER*
Take -away	**26**		**Burger King Drive Through Tel.01418-836239** A736 > Hillington, on the roundabout Open 8am-Midnight. Full Burger King menu. Drive through & restaurant.
Pub Grub / Restaurant	**26**	BREWERS FAYRE	**The Hillington Tel. 01418-101011** > Hillington Rd to Hillington Industrial Estate Pub is on r'bout. Our delicious menu provides a wide selection of value for money meals, as well as our own "daily specials". We look forward to welcoming you. Baby changing facilities. Toddler area. Childrens Parties. Disabled facilities. *SPECIAL OFFER*
FUEL	**27**	Shell	**Shell, Arkleston Tel.0141-889-7695** East Bound only, A741 > Renfrew, @ roundabout on L. OPEN 24 hrs, Shell Select Shop, with microwave snacks, Jet wash.air & water.
Pub Grub	**27**		**The Abbot's Inch Tel.0141-886-4988 Fax.885-2888** A741 > Paisley, opposite you as you come off the motorway. Coffee & Home baking served from 10 am. Bar food and restaurant.

	Exit		
SUPER STORE **FUEL**	27	TESCO	**Tesco Super Store, Renfrew Tel.01418-863795** A741 > Renfrew, 0.5m R > Newmains Rd. Petrol Station open 8am - 8.30 pm. (Sun 8am-6pm.) Facilities at this Super Store include:- No coffee shop or special facilities at present
Hotel	28/ 29		**Forte Posthouse Hotel Tel. 01418 871212** > Glasgow Airport. Business class hotel offering unrivalled personal service.
Take -away	29		**Bon Appetit** A726 > Paisley, Ist R on the old road. Mobile Open 6-2.30, weekdays. Burgers. Baked spuds.Toasties. Chips etc
Hotel	30		**Forte Posthouse Erskine Tel.01418-120123 Fax.127642** > M898 take the 1st junction & turn R. Modern 166 bedroom hotel with full leisure club and excellent parking.
Relax	30		**Princess Louise Scottish Hospital Tel.01418-121100** > M898 on the roundabout. Craft Shop, Garden Centre, Furniture workshop and Cafe.

	Exit		
FUEL	4	BP	**B.P Service Station Tel.01506-843302** A803 > Linlithgow, 2.5m on R. OPEN 24 hours. with shop.
Relax	4		**Linlithgow Palace & St Michaels Church.** A 803 > Linlithgow, in the town centre, follow signs. (3.6m) A fine ruin in dramatic setting.with very interesting Church.
Pub Grub	4		**The Bridge Inn Tel.01506-842777** A803 > Linlithgow, on R (2.5m.) Ideal for lunches or evening meals, Car park at rear.
FUEL	4	Gulf	**Avon Filling Station** A803 > Linlithgow, 2.5m. on L. OPEN 24 hrs. All Fuels. Small shop. Car wash.
Relax	4		**Klondyke Garden Centre Tel.01324-711122** A9 > Falkirk, on L. Coffee shop open 9.30am - 4.45pm daily, Wide ranging Garden Centre.
Pub Grub	5		**The Ellwyn Tel.01324-483142** A905, > Grangemouth, R @ mini roundabout & R again at Traffic Lights. Open 12-2.30,5-7,(8pm Fri & Sat) Bar & Restaurant, Kids menu.
Take -away	5		**The Happy Haggis Tel.01324-483561** A905 > Grangemouth, R @ roundabout, & R again at Traffic Lights. Open 11.30am -1.30 & 4-11pm. Fish & Chips, Haggis, Sweets & Drinks.
CAMPING	9		**Auchenbowie Caravan & Camping Site Tel.01324-822141** A 872 > Denny, Follow signs, 1m. Open Apr-Oct. Off the road and very quiet. Very pleasant.
			Please remember to mention "Just Off..." **when you visit one of our locations**

	Exit		
Pub Grub / Restaurant	9	(Brewery Fayre logo)	**Pirnhall Inn Tel. 01786-811256** A872 > Stirling. (.3m Off) Our delicious menu provides a wide selection of value for money meals, as well as our own "daily specials". We look forward to welcoming you. Baby changing facilities. Garden. Childrens Parties. Outdoor play equipment. Disabled facilities. Accommodation. Breakfasts. *(SPECIAL OFFER)*
Relax	10		**Stirling Castle & Visitor Centre. Tel.01786-50000** > Stirling, follow the signs. Open Apr -Sept 9.30am-6pm, Oct-March 9.30am-5pm
REPAIRS	10	ATS.	**A.T.S.** > Stirling, 1m on R. Open 8am-5pm & Saturday morning. Tyres & Exhausts.
FUEL	10	BURMAH	**Kildean Auto Point Tel.01786-462593 Fax.462593** > Stirling on L. OPEN 24hrs. All fuels. Shop with microsnacks. Toilets. Gas. Car wash.
Take-away	10		**China City Tel.01786-445596** > Stirling, through the lights on the L. Chinese Food. You may ring your order in.
B&B	10		**Kings Park Farm Tel.01786-474142** > Stirling, 1st R. > Castle, L @ roundabout on R. B&B with drink facilities.Family rooms. Fine views.10mins town centre.
Restaurant	10		**The Riverway Restaurant Tel.01786-475734** > Stirling, on L by Burmah Fuel. Open Wed - Sun. 10.30-6.30, Coffee,light meals,Trad.Scottish High Tea.

	Exit		
FUEL	7	Shell	**Shell Service Station** A11 > Harlow 0.3m on L. OPEN 24 hrs. Shell Select Shop with microwave snacks and ice creams.
Take-away	7		**Martin's Snacks Tel.01992-769495** > B1393 Epping. Mobile Open Mon-Sat 7am-4pm.in layby. All fresh food and drinks.
Restaurant	7	(Little Chef logo)	**Little Chef Tel.01279-4170157** A11 > Harlow 0.3m. on L. Open 7am-10pm..Licensed, baby change & disabled facilities. Coffee Stop. Fuel.
Hotel	8		**Stansted Airport Motel Tel.01279-871777 Fax.870746** A120 > Dunmow 3.9 miles on the L Friendly owner operated Motel, all rooms en suite, TV etc.. Book ahead.
FUEL	8		**Start Hill Service Stn. Tel.01279-503959** A120 > Colchester 100 yds on L. OPEN 24 hrs. Shop with microwave snacks, & Coffee.
Pub Grub	8		**The Nags Head Tel.01279-654553** A1250 > B' Stortford, > town centre 1m on L. Bar open 11-3 & 5.30-11, Non smoking family room, Steaks a speciality.

REMEMBER – Tiredness kills – TAKE A BREAK

	Exit		
Pub Grub	8		**The Green Man Tel.01279-870367** A120 > Dunmow 1.7m on L. This is a 300 year old pub with a friendly atmosphere. Traditional ales and a variety of delicious well-presented home-made meals. We have a good selection of vegetarian dishes and a variety of childrens' choices. COFFEE SERVED ALL DAY. Meals served every day 11-3 & 7-9.30. Open all day Fri, Sat, Sun.
Service Area / Hotel	8	Shell / LITTLE CHEF	**Welcome Break, Birchanger Green Services. Tel.01279-653388 Fax.652490** Follow the signs off the motorway Granary self service restaurant, shop, phones, travel information. Events arena. Little Chef, baby change and disabled facilities. Travel lodge. Julie's Pantry, K F C.,Sbarro Italian Restaurant & a Caffe Primo. Shell fuels, water & air.
FUEL	10	BP	**Duxford Service Stn., Tel.01223-832412 Fax.837326** A505 > Royston, 0.5m on R. Fuel 7am-9pm. (Sun 9-6) also full workshop facilities..
FUEL	10	TEXACO	**Aerodrome Service Stn., Tel.01223-833837** A505 > Royston, 300 yds. Open 6am-10pm. All fuels, small shop, air & water.
Relax	10		**Imperial War Museum, Tel.01223-835000** A505 > Royston 200 yds. on L. Open all year @ 10am. 140 aircraft on display, Restaurant.
Hotel	10		**The Red Lion Hotel Tel.01223-832047 Fax.837576** A505 > Newmarket, 1.5 miles. 13th C beautiful Hotel is open all day. 18 bedrooms are en-suite. Coaches welcome.
B&B	11		**Friarswood B&B. Tel.01223-841294** A10 > Cambridge, > Airport sign on R. 1.5m from Motorway. Beautiful large town house with large garden.
Relax	12		**Lay By** A603 > Sandy on L just before village A quiet lay by behind a hedge just outside the village on right hand corner.
Pub Grub	12		**The White Horse Inn, Tel.01223-262327** >A603 Sandy. on R. in village. (0.8m from Motorway). Large Garden, Featured in Cambridge good Food Guide. Open 12-2.30 & 6.30-11
CAMPING	12		**High Field Farm Camping Park Tel.01223-262308 Fax.262308** A603 > Sandy, for 0.5m. then R > B1046 Comberton follow signs. Beautiful 8 acre award winning park, Vans & Tents, hook ups, showers.
FUEL	12	Q8	**Wallis & Son Ltd., Tel;01223-263911 Fax.262912** A603 > Bedford, 1m on L. Open 7am -10pm (Sun 8-10) All Fuels, Workshop facilities, Car wash.
Pub Grub / Restaurant	13	BREWERS FAYRE	**Churchill Tel. 01223-365025** > Cambridge (1 m Off) Our delicious menu provides a wide selection of value for money meals, as well as our own "daily specials". We look forward to welcoming you. Baby changing facilities.Toddler area. Garden. Childrens Parties. Outdoor play equipment.

Please remember to mention "Just Off..." when you visit one of our locations

Cafe Diner	1		**Hot Stuff Cafe Tel.01709-703499** A631 > Bawtry, 1st L into Ind Estate, Follow sign to L. Open 7.30am-2pm. Clean, warm, Hot & Cold food & drink.Eat in or out.
Take-away	1		**Blank Bramley Fisheries** A631 > Rotherham, 0.5m R @ 2nd lights 200yds on R. FISH & CHIPS.
Restaurant	1	LITTLE CHEF	**Little Chef Tel.01709-545466** A631 > Bramley, Double back @ 2nd Junction, on L. Open 7am-10pm Full Little Chef menu.Licensed. Fuel..
FUEL	1	FINA	**White Rose Service Stn. Tel.01709-540877** A631 > Bramley, Double back @ 2nd junction on L. Open 7am-10pm (Sun8-10), All fuels & shop with cold drinks.
Hotel	1		**Hotel Grill Campanile Tel.01709-700255 Fax.545169** A631 > Bawtry, 1st L. into Ind. Estate, 2nd L. Restaurant & Bistro. Fine modern Hotel.
Restaurant	3		**Big Pan Pizza** Follow signs to racecourse, then Leisure Park.close to Warner Cinema.(4.2m Off)
Pub Grub Restaurant	3	BREWERS FAYRE	**Cheswold Tel. 01302-533000** *SPECIAL OFFER* Follow signs to racecourse, then Leisure Park.next to Warner Cinema. (4.2m Off). Our delicious menu provides a wide selection of value for money meals, as well as our own "daily specials". We look forward to welcoming you. Baby changing facilities.Toddler area. Fun Factory. Garden. Childrens Parties. Outdoor play equipment. Disabled facilities.
Take-away	3		**Mcdonalds Drive Through** Follow signs to racecourse, then Leisure Park.next to Warner Cinema. (4.2m Off) Sited in Modern Retail Pleasure Park with full Big Mac service
Service Area	3		**ASDA** Follow signs to racecourse, then Leisure Park. FUEL, Cafe, Dry cleaning, Open 9am-10pm (Sat 8.30-8, Sun 10-4)
FUEL	4	JET	**A. Binks Service Station Tel.01302-834700** A630 > Doncaster, L. @ roundabout, 1m. Open 7am-9pm. (Sat 8-8, Sun 9-6). All fuels and small shop.
Take-away	4		**Atlantic Fisheries** A630 > Doncaster L @ roundabout, Open 11.30-1.30,5-11.30 (closed Sun) Fish & Chips, Kebabs
Cafe Diner	6		**The Delves** > Thorne 1m on the R. Home made food, snacks & cakes by the lake, Good parking but no HGV.

REMEMBER – Tiredness kills – TAKE A BREAK

Cafe Diner Take-away	2		**Oak Dene Cafe Tel.01732-884873** Follow the signs to the services. Open Monday to Friday 6 am - 6.30 pm, Sat 6.30 am to 5 pm, Sun 8 am to 2 pm. Trucks and cars all welcome. All day breakfast, Dinners etc., Breakfast only at weekends. plus Take-away service.
SUPER STORE FUEL	4	TESCO	**Tesco Super Store, Aylesford Tel.01622-718016** A228 > Rochester, R @ 1st roundabout, 0.5 m. on R. Petrol Station open 6am-12pm. Facilities at this Super Store include:- Coffee Shop. toilets.
Pub Grub	4		**The Bricklayers Arms, Tel.01622-718151** A228 Rochester, R @ 1st roundabout >New Hythe L @ next roundabout, on R. Coffee served all day, Full menu and bar snacks.
Take-away	4		**Ali's Place, Tel.01474-814091** A228 > Rochester, across roundabout, 300yds on L in Layby. Mobile, all day fast food. Open 6am-5pm.
Cafe Diner	4		**The Town House Cafe, Tel.01732-874100** A228 > Tonbridge R @ 1st roundabout, L @ 2nd roundabout,on R in High St. Open all day, (Closed Sun.) Full all day breakfast, Good home cooking
Restaurant	4		**Gandhi Tandoori Tel.0177732-845600** A338 > Tonbridge, R @ 1st roundabout, L @ 2nd roundabout, >W.Malling, on R Open 12-2.30 & 6-12pm. Indian & English dishes, Restaurant & Take away.
Hotel	5		**Beefeater Travel Inn Tel.01622-752515** A20 > Maidstone, 0.7 m on R. Coffee all day, Bar snacks etc., All rooms en suite TV hot drinks.
SUPER STORE	5		**J.Sainsbury Plc.** A20 > Aylesford, 1 m. on L. Open for all fuels 7am-9pm (Sun. 7-6)
Hotel	7		**Stakis Hotel, Maidstone Tel.01622-734322** A249 > Maidstone, R @ roundabout, Hotel is on the R. ****Hotel, 24 hour reception, leisure facilities, 139 rooms en suite.
REPAIRS	7		**Kentish Bell Garages Tel.01622-737473** A249 > Sheerness, 1st. R > Detling,in village on R. Open 8am-7pm. Full workshop, all types of work done.
Pub Grub	7		**The Cock Horse, Tel.01622-737092** A249 > Sheerness, R in Detling, on left @ top of hill. Parking @ rear. Open for coffee & drinks All Day,Food 12-2.15 & 6.30-9.15.
SUPER STORE FUEL	7	TESCO	**Tesco Super Store, Maidstone Tel.01622-631469** A249 > Maidstone, L @ roundabout,R @ next & L @ next. 500yds on R. Petrol Station open 6.30am - 11pm. Facilities at this Super Store include:- Coffee Shop. Baby changing and toilets.
Take-away	9		**Vincent's Snacks. Tel.01233-630470** A20 > Tenterden, 400yds in layby on L. Open Mon - Fri 8am-4pm. Hot & Cold drinks sandwiches etc.,

Hotel	9		**Ashford International Hotel, Tel.01233-219988** A28 > Canterbury, L @ 1st roundabout, 200yds on L. **** Modern Hotel, Restaurants, Bars, Conference & Leisure facilities.
SUPER STORE	9		**J.Sainsbury Plc.** A28 > Canterbury, L @ roundabout L @ lights. Open 7am - 9pm. All Fuels, Cafe in store.
Hotel	10		**Warren Cottage Tel.01233 621905 Fax.623400** B2164 > Canterbury (Kennington Rd,) R at first roundabout. A privately owned hotel set in two acres of gardens. 3 Crown ETB commended. The bedrooms all have private facilities and colour TV. Large car park. Restaurant open 6.30 - 10pm. Bar all day. Minutes from Ashford international station , the Channel Tunnel and ports.
Pub Grub	10		**The White Horse, Tel.01233-624257** B2164 > Canterbury. 0.5 m on L. Home cooked food, Kids welcome, Open11am-3 &5.30-11pm
Hotel	10		**Master Spearpoint Hotel Tel.01233-636863 Fax.610119** B2164 > Canterbury, R @ end of road, 10 yds on R. ** Country House Hotel, 24hr.porter, Rooms en suite.(Tunnel 10 mins)
SUPER STORE FUEL	10	TESCO	**Tesco Super store, Ashford Tel.01233-500010** Follow the signs for Super Store. Petrol Station OPEN 24 hours. Facilities at this Super Store include:- Coffee Shop. Baby changing and toilets.
CAMPING	11		**Folkston Racecourse Tel. 01303-261761** A261 > Hythe, & A20 r'bout > Sellindge, then R > Racecourse. (1.6m Off) Caravan Club site open 12 Apl- 9th oct (8am - 8pm) 4 acres, 60 pitches.
Pub Grub	11		**The Drum Inn Tel.01303-812125** B2068 > Canterbury, > 1st. exit on L. On R. 300year old Inn, in quiet village, Food 12am-2 & 7-8.45pm.
Restaurant	12	LITTLE CHEF	**Little Chef Tel.01303-279878** A 20 > Cheriton, 1st L & L again. Open 7am-10pm. Full Little Chef menu, shop & toilets. disabled facilities.
SUPER STORE FUEL	12	TESCO	**Tesco Super Store, Folkestone Tel.01622-631469** A20 > Cheriton, 1st R on R. in High street. Petrol Station OPEN 24 hour. Facilities at this Super Store include:- Coffee Shop. Baby changing and toilets.
Take-away	12		**The Seafarer Tel.01303-275185** A20 > Cheriton, 500yds on R. Fish & Chip Takeaway, Clean & Friendly, Mon-Sat. 11.30am-2pm & 5-11pm.
Pub Grub Restaurant	13	BREWERS FAYRE	**Brickfield Tel. 01303-273619** > Folkstone Rd, beside the Burger King. Our delicious menu provides a wide selection of value for money meals, as well as our own "daily specials". We look forward to welcoming you. Baby changing facilities. Fun Factory. Garden. Childrens Parties. Outdoor play equipment. Disabled facilities. Accommodation. Breakfasts.

M23	Exit		*Outwood Post Mill has ground flour by wind since 1665 (east before Exit 9)*
FUEL	9	TEXACO	**Star Service Station. Tel.01293-511131** > road to North terminal, across 1st roundabout, 3rd exit on 2nd roundabout. OPEN 24 HOURS. Large shop selling. Hot Fast Foods, Newspapers, Dunkin Donuts, and lots more shopping.
Hotel	9		**The Gatwick Travel Inn Hotel, Tel.01293-568158 Fax.568278** > N.Terminal, across 1st roundabout, 3rd exit on 2nd roundabout, 150yds on R 24hr reception.Restaurant, All rooms en suite, 2 Meeting Rooms.
SUPER STORE **FUEL**	10	TESCO	**Tesco Super Store, Crawley Tel.01293-562652** A264 > Crawley, 1.3m, 1st exit @ roundabout on L. Petrol Station OPEN 24 hours. Facilities at this Super Store include:- Coffee Shop Baby changing and toilets.
B&B	10		**Kitsbridge House, Tel.01342-714422** A264 > E.Grinstead, L @ 1st. roundabout, 2nd house on R. All rooms tea & coffee,TV, Showers. Light Breakfast.
Pub Grub *Restaurant*	11	BREWERS FAYRE	**Mill House Tel. 01293-534959** A23 > Crawley, 500 yds from Ifield Golf Club.(2.5m Off) Our delicious menu provides a wide selection of value for money meals, as well as our own "daily specials". We look forward to welcoming you. Baby changing facilities. Play Zone. Garden. Childrens Parties. Outdoor play equipment. Disabled facilities. (SPECIAL OFFER)
Service Area	11	Shell LITTLE CHEF	**Welcome Break, Pease Pottage Services. Tel.01293-562852** Follow the signs off the motorway Granary self service restaurant, Little Chef and Travel Lodge, baby change and disabled facilities shop, phones, games, and toilets. Shell fuels, water & air.

M25	Exit		*Quebec House, (SW of Exit 5) Jacobean House, commemorates General Wolffe, killed 1759*
Service Area	S		**Road Chef, Clacket Lane Services. Tel.01959-565577** Road Chef restaurant, Shop & Lodge, Tourist Info Centre. Wimpey (open 10-10) Cash Dispensers. Foot bridge connects East & West bound.
Pub Grub *Restaurant*	4	BREWERS FAYRE	**Badgers Mount Tel. 01959-534777** A21 >Bromley, 1st exit @ 1st R'bout, over next r'bout on R. Our delicious menu provides a wide selection of value for money meals, as well as our own "daily specials". We look forward to welcoming you. Baby changing facilities. Fun Factory. Garden. Childrens Parties. Outdoor play equipment. Disabled facilities. (SPECIAL OFFER)
Hotel	8		**Bridge House Hotel & Restaurant. Tel.01737-246801 Fax.223756** A217 > Reigate, 0.3m on R. Fine Views, All rooms ensuite, Restaurant open 12.30-2.15 & 7.30-12.
Pub Grub	8		**The Yew Tree, Tel.01737-244944** A217 > Reigate, Down hill 1m on R. Open 11am-11pm. Food and coffee all day, Kids welcome, Beer Garden.

Relax	8		**Free Parking with Views.** A217 > Reigate, 1st.L, follow the signs. Beautiful views of Reigate and airport, Toilets & icecream kiosk.
SUPER STORE **FUEL**	9	IIIIIII TESCO	**Tesco Super Store, Leatherhead Tel.01372-363633** A244 > Leatherhead into Oxshott Rd. Petrol Station open 8.30am - 9 pm. (Sun 9am-5pm.) Facilities at this Super Store include:- Baby changing toilets.
Cafe Diner	10		**Gale's Diner, Tel.01932-867717** A3 > Guildford, 400yds on L at the layby. Open 8am-4.30pm.(Sat Sun 9-5) Fastfood Take-away. All day breakfast.
Relax	10		**Relax in the layby (Cafe)** A3 > Guildford, 400yds on L. Fishing, Picnic area, Semaphore tower ! Toilets.
FUEL	10	**MURCO**	**Murco Tel.01932-865399** A3 > London, >A245 Leatherhead, up slip road, 400yds on L. Open 24 hrs. All fuels, Car wash, Shop with microwave snacks.
Hotel	10		**The Hautboy, Tel.01483-225355** A3 > Guildford,1st L.>B2039 Ockham, 1st L on R. (2.7m from motorway). Highly Recommended, Built 1864, All rooms ensuite TV etc., Restaurant
Pub Grub	11		**Woburn Arms Tel.01932-563314** A314 > Weybridge, 2nd exit @ roundabout, 150yds on L. Open for Bar snacks 11am-11pm.Kids welcome, Conference facilities.
FUEL	17	BP	**Polygon Millend Express Tel.01923-778446** A412 > Rickmansworth, L @ roundabout, o.25m on R. OPEN 24 hrs. Large shop, microwave, & car wash. All fuels.
FUEL	18	Shell	**Shell Chorleywood Service Stn. Tel.01582-285031** A404 > Amersham, 500yds on R. OPEN 24 hrs. All fuels, jet wash, shop with microwave and coffee.
Pub Grub	18		**The White Horse Tel.01923-282227 Fax.282227** A404 > Amersham, 500 yds. on L. Open 11-3 & 5.30-11. Traditional English Pub. Bar snacks & full menu. Garden.
Pub Grub	20		**The Kings Head Tel.01923-262307** A41 > Watford, L @ lights 200yds on R. parking @ rear. Open 11-4 & 5-11. Families welcome. Garden by canal. Food & ale well recommended
FUEL	20	FINA	**Hunton Bridge Service Station Tel.01923-267964** A41 > Watford 0.5m on L. OPEN 24 hrs. All fuels, jet wash. Coffee & microwave in shop.
Pub Grub	20		**Langleys Homespread Tel.01923 263150** A4521 > Kings Langley, through high St. on L after church. Open all day, families welcome, Funky Forrest play area, good food & Lodge Inn.
B&B	21a		**The Old Schoolhouse Tel.01727-874239 Fax.874275** A405 >St Albans,over M25, R @ roundabout, R @ end of road, 50yds on R, on corner. Basins and drinks trays in double/family rooms. No smoking. Excellent reputation. Five minutes walk from town centre & station to London. Good local services.Each room is centrally heated and has refrigerator, microwave, & colour TV. We strongly advise that you ring ahead.

Relax	22		**Bowmans Open Farm Tel.01727-822106 Fax.826406** Follow signs from the junction, Working open farm with trail, fishing, pets corner, shop and licensed restaurant.
SUPER STORE	22		**J.Sainsbury Plc. Sava Centre** A1081 > London Colney, 2nd L. @ roundabout. Open 6am-9pm, All fuels, coffee shop in the main store.
Service Area	23	BP / LITTLE CHEF	**Welcome Break, South Mimms Services. Tel.01707-646333** Follow the signs off the motorway Granary self service restaurant, shop, phones, games, and toilets. Little Chef and Travel Lodge, baby change and disabled facilities. Julie's Pantry, Sharro Italian Restaurant. BP fuels, water & air.
Hotel	24		**West Lodge Park Tel.01814-408311 Fax.493698** A111 > Cockfosters, 1.5m on L. English country mansion in 35 acre park.Beautifully furnished, fine restaurant.
Restaurant	24		**Akash Indian Restaurant Tel.01707-643778** A111 > Brookmans Park,0.5m on L. Open Lunch time & evenings till very late. Wide ranging menu.
REPAIRS	24		**Kwik Fit** A111 > Brookmans Park, L @ lights > A1000 50 yds on R. Full tyre service.
Restaurant	25	LITTLE CHEF	**Little Chef Tel.01992-630788** A10 > Cambridge. Open 7am-10pm. Full Little Chef menu, disabled facilities.
Relax	25		**Capel Manor Gardens Tel.01813-664442** A10 > Enfield, Follow the brown signs. Open daily in the summer months. 10am - 5.30pm, last entry at 4.30pm. Admission Fee. Beautiful and instructional with a wide range of gardens. Farm corner, cafeteria and shop. Also available for conventions, business meetings & hospitality/promotion events.
FUEL	25		**Chesunt Service Station Tel.01992-636964** A10 > Cambridge. Open 7am-11pm. All fuels, jet wash, shop with microsnacks.
SUPER STORE FUEL	25	TESCO	**Tesco Super Store, Cheshunt Tel.01992-637385** A10 > Hertford > through roundabout to Brookfield Centre on L.(2.4m). Petrol Station OPEN 24 hours. Facilities at this Super Store include:- Dispensing Pharmacy, Cash dispenser. Baby changing and toilet
Pub Grub	26		**The Volunteer Tel.01992-713705** A121. Loughton, 150 yds. on R. Real ales.Traditional Pub, serving chinese style food and bar snacks.
Take-away	26		**Martins Snacks** > A121, under the M25 between the roundabouts Mobile Van, Open all night from 7pm-6am,for fresh food and drinks
Restaurant	26		**City Limits Bar & Restaurant** A121 > Loughton, 1m on L. American Theme Restaurant and Bar. Traditional '50s diner, serving great food.

Hotel	26		**Swallow Hotel Tel.01992-711841** A121 > Waltham Abbey, R @ roundabout. **** Hotel. A fine modern hotel with leisure club & quality accommodation.
Pub Grub	26		**The Woodbine Inn Tel.01992-713050** A121 > Loughton, 200 yds on L. Open all day, Food 11am-3pm. Bar menu & snacks. Families welcome.
FUEL	28	FINA	**South Weald Service Station Tel.01277-833819** A1023 > Brentwood, 50 yds on L. OPEN 24 hrs. All fuels, car wash.
Restaurant	28	LITTLE CHEF	**Little Chef Tel.01277-201519** A1023 > Brentwood, 50 yds on L. Open 7am-10pm. Full Little Chef Menu, Licensed, disabled facilities. Fuel.
B&B	29		**The Brick House Hotel Tel.01277 217107** A127 > Southend, 0.25m on L. on the B186. > Brentwood. 3 miles Brentwood Station or 3 miles Upminster Underground station.
SUPER STORE **FUEL**	29	TESCO	**Tesco Super Store, Basildon Tel.01268-522731** A127, the store on your R. continue to slip Rd. & come back. Petrol Station open 6am. - 10pm. (Sun. 8am- 8pm.) Facilities at this Super Store include:- Coffee Shop. Home and Wear. Baby changing and toilets.
Relax	30		**Lakeside Shopping Centre** On the service area roundabout take the third exit, B186 > West Thurrock, Reputed to be the largest indoor shopping mall in Europe.open10am-10pm.
Take -away	30		**McDonalds** On the service area roundabout take the third exit, B186 > West Thurrock, Full McDonald's Menu, Drive through.
SUPER STORE	30	TESCO	**Tesco Super Store. Thurrock** On the service area roundabout take the third exit, B186 > West Thurrock, 1st L Petrol Station OPEN 24 hours. Facilities at this Super Store include :- Coffee Shop. Dispensing Pharmacy, Cash dispenser. Baby changing and toilets.
B&B	30		**Stifford Clays Farm House Tel.01375 375918** A13> South End @ 2nd Exit A1012> North bound 1st R & R into Stifford Clays Rd. Good value accommodation.all rooms en suite,TV etc. Book ahead.
Restaurant *Hotel*	30		**The Old Clock Carvery & Hotel Tel.01708-865102 Fax.890131** > Aveley, into village > R on L. Our evening A La Cart restaurant is open Wed, Thur, Fri. Carvery open Sat eve & Sunday Lunch time. This is a small, personal restaurant with wide ranging menu. (Skillet, Balti, Corma meals & traditional Steaks.) You are advised to book ahead for accommodation.
Service Area	30/31	**ESSO**	**Granada, Thurock Services. Tel.01708-865487** Follow the signs. Tourist Information Centre. Restaurant, Burger King, Photos. Shop, Granada Lodge.
Pub Grub Restaurant	31	BREWERS FAYRE	**Chafford Hundred Tel. 01375-481153** Next to Safeways, .5m from Lakeside Shopping centre, via tunnel under railway. Our delicious menu provides a wide selection of value for money meals, as well as our own "daily specials". We look forward to welcoming you. Baby changing facilities. Fun Factory. Garden. Childrens Parties. Outdoor play equipment. Disabled facilities. SPECIAL OFFER

North of this road is Lullingstone Villa, Roman, 1800 years old and well preserved

Pub Grub	2		**The Moat Beefeater, Tel.01732-882263** A20 > London 0.7 m on L. Open 10.30am -11pm. Full lunch menu, Bar snacks during afternoon.
FUEL	2	**TOTAL**	**Petropolis Tel.01732-780132** A20 > London, 0.5m on R. Open 24hr. All Fuels, car wash, Shop with Microwave snacks.
Cafe Diner Take -away	2		**Oak Dene Cafe, Tel;01732-884152** Follow the signs to the services. Trucks and cars all welcome, All day breakfast, Dinners etc., Open Monday to Friday 6 am - 6.30 pm. Saturday 6.30 am - 5 pm, Sunday 8 am - 2 pm. Breakfasts only at weekends plus take-away service.

Paulton's Park (Exit 2) with pink flamingoes, rare breeds and Roman Museum

Take -away	2		**McDonald's Tel.01703-814487** A36 > Salisbury, across roundabout, behind petrol station. Full McDonald's Menu, Drive through.
FUEL	2	TEXACO	**Star, West Wellow Tel.01703-814541** A36 > Salisbury, across roundabout, (only 500 yds from motorway.) Open 24 hrs. All Fuels, Car wash, Shop, Microwave snacks.
Service Area	S	**ESSO**	**Road Chef, Rownhams Services. Tel.01703-734480** Follow the signs from the motorway. Road Chef restaurant and shop, toilets etc.
Pub Grub Restaurant	3	BREWERS FAYRE	**The Gateway Tel. 01703-650541** > A335 R at lights. (100yds Off.) Our delicious menu provides a wide selection of value for money meals, as well as our own "daily specials". We look forward to welcoming you. Baby changing facilities.Toddler area. Garden. Outdoor play equipment. Accommodation. Breakfasts. (SPECIAL OFFER)
SUPER STORE	7		**J.Sainsbury Plc.** Follow signs to super store. Fuel Open 7am-10pm (Sun 8-6) All fuels, Car wash, Barclays Cash,
FUEL	7	TEXACO	**Thornhill Service Stn., Tel.01703-470181** A334 > Southampton, (0.75m.) Texaco 24 hour,All fuels,Car & Jet wash,Hot snacks,Toilets,Free air.
Pub Grub Restaurant	8	BREWERS FAYRE	**Windhover Manor Tel. 01703-403500** > Hamble. Opposite Tesco @ Bursledon roundabout. Our delicious menu provides a wide selection of value for money meals, as well as our own "daily specials". We look forward to welcoming you. Baby changing facilities.Toddler area. Garden. Childrens Parties. Outdoor play equipment. Disabled facilities. (SPECIAL OFFER)
REPAIRS	8		**Sunday Hill MOT Centre, Tel.01703-406944** > Hedge End, over hill on L. MOT's and all mechanical repairs.Open 8-5 Mon -Fri (Sat 8-12)

Please remember to mention "Just Off..."
when you visit one of our locations

SUPER STORE **FUEL**	8	||||||| TESCO	**Tesco Super Store, Bursledon Tel.01703-405144** A3024 > Southampton East, 2nd exit @ roundabout > Hamble Lane. Petrol Station open 6am. - midnight. Facilities at this Super Store include:- Coffee Shop. Dispensing Pharmacy, Cash dispenser. Baby changing and toilets.
Relax	8		**Manor Farm, Hedge End.** > Hedge End, 2nd R, only 500yds from motorway Beautifully managed woodlands with parking, (Charges during summer)
FUEL	8	M⊙bil	**Sundays Hill Petrol Stn. Tel.01703-405958** > Hedge End, over hill, 0.5m on L Open 6am-10pm, All fuels, small shop, air & water.
Hotel	9		**Solent Hotel Tel.01489-880000 Fax.880007** > Business Park. L @ roundabout. ****Hotel. conference facilities, Leisure club, All facilities.
Pub Grub	9		**The Parson's Collar Tel.01489-880035** > Business Park, L @ roundabout Open 11-2.30 & 5-11. Carvery style lunches, Full evening meals.
Restaurant	9		**T.G.I. Friday's American Bistro Tel.01489-577533 Fax.589735** A27 > Farnham,across roundabout. Open 12-11pm, American Bistro, Wide range of food and drink served.
cAMPIng	11		**Farham Country Club Tel.01329-822248 Fax.822248** A27 >Portchester,L after viaduct,L @ 2nd lights, Follow signs. Hotel, Tents & Vans, Fitness & Health Suite, Squash, Bar & Restaurant.
Hotel	11		**The Roundabout Hotel, Tel.01329-822542 Fax.234533** A27 > Farnham L @ slip Rd. Last exit on roundabout pub on R. Some rooms en suite,TV & Drinks. Bar & Restaurant open all day.
Pub Grub Restaurant	12	BREWERS FAYRE	**Ship & Castle Tel. 01705-832009** M275 > Portsmouth then follow the signs to Historic Ships, the pub is opposite. Our delicious menu provides a wide selection of value for money meals, as well as our own daily specials'. We look forward to welcoming you. Baby changing facilities.Toddler area. Play Zone. Childrens Parties. Disabled facilities.

Hotel	1		**Forte Crest Hotel. Tel.01179-564242 Fax.,9569735** > Filton & Parkway, 700yds 0n L. **** Hotel, 200 rooms, Conference facilities, 24 hr. night porter.
Take -away	2		**Fast Burgers, Unit 6. Tel.01272-354288** B4469 > Southmead, 100yds on L. Open 10am- 11pm. for Fast Burgers, Shakes, Hot & Cold Drinks.
FUEL	2	Shell	**Shell Eastville Park Tel.01179-580000** B4469 >Fish Pond. 200 yds on R OPEN 24 hrs, Shell Select Shop, microwave snacks, ice creams, car wash & vacuum.
			REMEMBER – Tiredness kills – TAKE A BREAK

	Exit		
REPAIRS	1	ATS	**ATS Tyres & Exhausts. Tel.01895-233705** A40 > Uxbridge, 1m on R. Open 8.30am-5.30pm All tyres and Batteries
Pub Grub	1		**The Lambert Arms Tel.01895-255613** > Uxbridge,.25m on L. Breakfast 7-10am, Lunch 12-2pm. Evening Meal 6-9pm Tues-Sat.
FUEL	1	Mobil	**Prime Garages Ltd., Tel.01895-832221** A40 > Gerrards Cross,.5m on L. OPEN 24 hr. Car wash, Toilet, Microwave snacks & coffee
Pub Grub Restaurant	2	BREWERS FAYRE	**Magpies Tel. 01494-726754** A355 > Amersham, on L. (2 m Off.) Our delicious menu provides a wide selection of value for money meals, as well as our own "daily specials". We look forward to welcoming you. Baby changing facilities. Garden. Childrens Parties. Outdoor play equipment. Disabled facilities. — SPECIAL OFFER
Hotel	2		**The De Vere Bell House Hotel Tel.01753-887211** A40 >Beaconsfield R @ roundabout > Gerrards Cross 1m on R. **** hotel with leisure club, 2 restaurants, all rooms ensuite etc.
Hotel Restaurant	2	TOBY RESTAURANTS	**The White Hart Toby Hotel. Tel.01494-671211 Fax.670704** A40 > Beaconsfield, 1m in village > New town, on R. 16th. C. Hotel and Restaurant, bar food available all day. All rooms are en suite, with TV, hospitality tray, & trouser press. 5 function / meeting rooms Traditional Sunday lunches all day in restaurant, Another fine Toby Hotel - where Quality meets Tradition !
CAMPING	3		**Chapel Lane, Wythall Tel. 01564-826483** A435 > Birmingham, L & r'bout, then L into Chapel Lane. (1.75m Off.) Open all year, 8am - 8pm. Caravan Club site open to non-members.
Pub Grub Restaurant	4	BREWERS FAYRE	**Spade Oak Tel. 01628 520090** A404 > Maidenhead, @ 1st exit A4155> Bourne End R > Coldmoorholme Lane. (4m Off). Our delicious menu provides a wide selection of value for money meals, as well as our own "daily specials". We look forward to welcoming you. Baby changing facilities. Garden. Childrens Parties. Disabled facilities. — SPECIAL OFFER
SUPER STORE	4		**Asda** A4010 > Aylesbury, L at the roundabout, on the L. (400yds Off.) FUEL, Cafe, Open 9am-10pm (Sat 8.30-8pm , Sun 10-4pm)
Restaurant	4		**Deep Pan Pizza Co., Tel.01494-4657067** A4010 > Aylesbury, 200yds on L. Open 12-12. All styles of Pizzas, Salads, Pasties. Licensed.
Hotel	4		**Forte Posthouse Tel.01494-442100 Fax. 439071** A4010 > Aylesbury, 100 yds on R. Modern Hotel with Restaurant, Leisure facilities & all rooms en suite.
Pub Grub	4		**Boulevard Tel.01494-461045 Fax.445508** A4010 > Aylesbury, 200yds on L. Full menu all day, Lively at night.
FUEL	5		**Tower Garage Tel.01494-484382** A40 > Stokenham, 400 yds on R. Open 6am-11pm. All Fuels, Car wash, Shop with microwave snacks.

	Exit		
Hotel Restaurant	5		**The Fox Country Hotel. Tel.01491-638722** > Ibstone, 1m. on L. I mile off Junction 5 through beautiful woodland in an area of outstanding natural beauty. 300 yr. old Inn, serves coffee, bar food, restaurant, real ales. Pretty patio & garden. Real log fires & beams. 9 en suite bedrooms. Sunday lunch specials, small meeting room, very peaceful location.
Pub Grub	5		**The Four Horse Shoes Tel.01494-482265** A40 > Stokenchurch, 0.5 m on R. OPEN for breakfast,Hot & cold food all day.Function room,kids welcome.
REPAIRS	5	**MURCO**	**Stokenchurch Service Centre Ltd., Tel.01494-483355** A40 > High Wycombe, 1m on the R. 24 hr recovery, Workshops, servicing & MOT's, All Fuels.
Pub Grub **B&B**	6		**The Fox & Hounds Tel.01491 612142** *(SPECIAL OFFER)* B4009 > Watlington, 3 miles.on R. 17th. Century Inn, recently refurbished. Bar snacks & restaurant. Large car park Morning coffee, excellent, extensive & unusual menu, hot'n spicy specialities. Trad. Sunday lunch. Open for food Mon-Sat 11-2.30 & 6-11, Sun 12-3 &7-10.30. MORE THAN JUST A PUB! also Function room for private bookings.
Pub Grub	6		**The Leathern Bottle Tel.01844-351482** B4009 > Watling, 1st R 300yds on L. (0.5m from M-way) 400 yrs. old. Trad. Pub, food served 12-2 pm & 7-930pm.
Hotel	6		**Lambert Arms Tel.01844-351496 Fax.353626** > Chinnor > R,A40 Postcombe & Thame. Specialising in day meetings and offering overnight accommodation.
Restaurant	8		**Harvester Restaurant Tel.01865 875270** A40 > Oxford, > R Wheatley. on the L Wholesome freshly prepared food, Char-grill Barbecue & Self service Salad cart.
B&B	8		**Julia's Kitchen Tel.01844 339631** A418 > Thame 1st slip Rd. on L. !min.from the motorway. Comfortable modern house twin or double rooms, plenty of off road parking.
SUPER STORE	8		**Asda Super Store** A40 > Oxford, R > Wheatley. on the L Super Store , Fuel, Baby change, No Coffee shop.Open 7-7 Fri & Sat 7-8,Sun 9-5.
Hotel	8		**Forte Travelodge. Tel.0800 850 950** A40 > Oxford, R > Wheatley. on the L All the comfort & high standard you'd expect. E.T.B. commended.
Cafe Diner	9		**Caravan Truck Stop Tel.01869-323361** > Oxford, 200yds on L in Layby. Open 24 hrs. 7 days per week. Hot & cold food and drink.
FUEL	9	Shell	**Shell Layby Tel.01869-351227** A 34 > Oxford,1.5m. L.(To return to the motorway is 5 m.) All Fuels Shop with microwave snacks. Lottery.
Service Area	10	**ESSO**	**Granada, Cherwell Valley Services. Tel.01869-346060** Follow the signs off the motorway. Restaurant, Burger King, shop, phones, Lottery, cash points, Granada Lodge,
			Please remember to mention "Just Off..." **when you visit one of our locations**

Pub Grub	10		**The Bear Inn, Souldern Tel.01869-346785** A43 > Northampton, L > B4100, Aynho, on B4100, (1.9m.) Traditional Free House. Open 11.30 am - 2.30pm & 6.30 - 11pm. Roast Sunday lunch a must. Serving Bar snacks, Lunches and Evening meals. Large garden and car park. Function room available for private bookings. Winter log fires.
REPAIRS	10		**Corner Garage, Tel.01869-345329** B430 > Middleton Stoney, 0.5m. on R. Open 8-6pm Full garage facilities, Repairs & servicing, All Fuels.
Pub Grub	10		**The Fox & Hound, Tel.01869-346883** B430 > Middleton Stoney, 600yds on L. Open 12-3 &7-11. Full menu & bar snacks, 200yr old Village Pub.
Take~away	11		**Burger King Drive Through.** A422 > Banbury, follow the A422 through 3 roundabouts, R at the 4th. (1.5 m.) Full Burger King Menu with restaurant and drive through facilities.
Relax	11		**Banbury Retail Shopping Park** A422 > Banbury, follow the A422 through 3 roundabouts, R at the 4th. (1.5 m.) Do It All, Charlie Brown Auto Centre, Currys, £stretcher, Comet.
CAMPING	11		**Towns End, Simcoes Farm Tel.o1295 750565** A361 > Daventry, R > Upper Wardington, L@ junction, last house on L (4.2 m.Off) Small camp site with fresh eggs for sale. Local pub close by.
SUPER STORE FUEL	11	IIIIIII TESCO	**Tesco Banbury Tel.** A422 > Banbury, follow the A422 through 3 roundabouts, R at the 4th. (1.5 m.) Petrol Station Facilities in this store include:- Coffee Shop, Baby changing,Toilets. Non dispensing pharmacy.
FUEL	11	ESSO	**Ermont Way Service Stn., Tel.01295-279989** > Banbury, > L. Thorpe Way Ind. Estate, 200yds on L. 24 hr All Fuels Shop with Microwave Snacks,Lottery.
Relax	12		**Heritage Motor Centre, Tel.01926-641188 Fax.641555** Follow the signs. Transport Museum of British Cars. Cafe, Picnic area, Entrance Fee.
B&B	12		**Mrs Stanton, Redlands Farm, Tel.01926-651241** > Gaydon, R > B4100 2.5 m, signed on L. Quiet location, Full breakfast, single, double & family rooms.
Pub Grub	12		**Gaydon Inn Tel.01926-640388** > Gaydon L @ Junction 400 yds on R. Open 11-3 &5-11 All day Fri & Sat.., Trad. Village Pub. with Garden.
FUEL	12	ESSO	**Gaydon Service Stn., Tel.01926-642278** > Gaydon, Junction 400yds on L. Open 6-Midnight, Jet wash, Shop & Bakery, Microwave & Hot Drinks.
REPAIRS	12		**C.B.Motors Tel.01926-640303** > Gaydon, L @ Junction >B4100 400yds on L. Open 8-5.30 (Sat 8-1). MOT's, Repairs, & Servicing.
			REMEMBER – Tiredness kills – TAKE A BREAK

Service Area	S	LITTLE CHEF / Mobil	**Welcome Break, Warwick Services. N. Bound Tel.01926-651681 Fax.651696** Follow the signs off the motorway Granary self service restaurant, shop, phones, games, and toilets. Little Chef and Travel Lodge, baby change and disabled facilities. La Baguette and Sharro Italian Restaurant. Mobil fuels, water & air.
Cafe Diner	15		**Taff's Diner, (Transport). Tel.01789-415336** >Stratford-o-A. around roundabout & return to Layby (4m back to M-way) Open 7am-2pm All day breakfast, Hot food & drinks. Clean & Tidy.
Hotel	15		**Hilton National Tel. 01926-499555 Fax.410020** A429 > Warwick on L. Fine, modern, high class hotel, Pool & fitness room.
B&B	15		**Lower Watchbury Farm, Tel.01926-624772** A429>C'cester through Barford, >L opp. Granville Arms, 2nd Farm on L Beautiful accommodation on working farm in peaceful location. All en-suite rooms with hostess trays & colour TV. Excellent farm house breakfast, large garden, local pubs for evening meals. Tourist board 2 crowns commended Farm Holiday Bureau member.
Pub Grub	15		**Joseph Arch, Tel.01926-624365** > A429 Stow, in village 1st on R over bridge. Normal pub hours, Home cooked foods always available, Beer Garden.
Cafe Diner	16		**Olde Pounde Cafe, Tel.01564-782970** A3400 >Stratford, 2m. on R. (Difficult return to motorway)' Open weekdays 8-4.30 Specialty Breakfasts. Ample portions.

Take-away	2		**Eureka Diner Tel.01956-456481** A441 > Birmingham 200 yds in layby on L. Mobile open 8-3 Mon -Sat. Hot and cold food & drinks
Hotel	2		**Westmead Hotel Tel.01214-451202 Fax.456163** A441 > Birmingham, R @ roundabout > Birmingham 1m on R. *** Hotel with fine bar & restaurant, ideal for business or pleasure.
REPAIRS	2		**Hopwood Service Station Tel.01214-451616** A441 > Birmingham, L @ roundabout, on R. Full garage workshop for repairs & servicing. Recovery service & shop.
Pub Grub / Restaurant	3	BREWERS FAYRE	**Village Inn Tel. 01527-67227** A43 5 > Evesham, R @ 2nd R'bout B4101> Beoley in village, (3m Off) Our delicious menu provides a wide selection of value for money meals, as well as our own "daily specials". We look forward to welcoming you. Baby changing facilities. Garden.
Pub Grub	3		**The Rose & Crown, Tel.01564-822166** A435,>Redditch, L.>portway, R & over bridge back down A435 on L. Clean friendly pub & restaurant, bar food garden & play area. Coaches by appointment
FUEL	3	FINA	**Weatheroaks Service Station Tel.01564-824685** A435 > Birmingham, 400yds on L. OPEN 24 hrs. All fuels and shop with microwave snacks etc.

Restaurant	3		**Portway Restaurant, Tel.01564-824794** > A435, > Redditch, 1st L over bridge double back 500 yds on L. Italian Food @ it's Finest, Booking essential, Credit cards accepted.
Restaurant	4		**McDonald's Tel.01217-336327** A34 > Birmingham, 0.5m on R. Full McDonald's restaurant menu & drive through.
Pub Grub	4		**The Plough Tel..01217-442942** A34. Birmingham, 0.75m on L. Open for food and drinks all day, Travel Inn.
SUPER STORE FUEL	4	IIIIIII TESCO	**Tesco Super Store, Solihull Tel.01217-333383** A34 > Birmingham, 0.25 m on R. Petrol Station OPEN 24 hours. Facilities at this Super Store include:- Coffee Shop, Home and Wear. Baby changing and toilets.
Pub Grub Restaurant	5	BREWERS FAYRE	**Orange Tree Tel. 01564-782458** A4141 > Warwick, in Chadwick End. (4m Off) Our delicious menu provides a wide selection of value for money meals, as well as our own 'daily specials'. We look forward to welcoming you. Baby changing facilities. Play Zone. Garden. Childrens Parties. Outdoor play equipment.
Relax	6		**The National Exhibition Centre.** Follow the signs off the motorway. There is nearly always something interesting going on.
Hotel	6		**Forte Posthouse Tel.01217-828141 Fax.822476** A45 > Birmingham, 2m. on the R. Restaurant, bar & Lounge serving 24hr food. Close to NEC, airport & Birmingham.
FUEL	6	ESSO	**Bickenhill Service Station Tel.01675-443485** A45 > Solihull, 1st L over bridge & double back 100yds on L. OPEN 24 hrs. for all fuels.
Pub Grub	6	TOBY RESTAURANTS	**The Maltshovel Tel.01675-442326** A45 > Coventry, 1st slip Rd. on L. L & roundabout, & L into car park. Open all day. Food 12-2.30 & 6-10.30. A bar/restaurant eating house, kids welcome
Relax	6		**National Motorcycle Museum Tel,01675-443311** Follow the signs from the exit. Museum with 700 motorcycles. Entrance Fee. Restaurant. Conference facilities.
Hotel Pub Grub	9		**Lea Marston Hotel & Leisure Complex. Tel.01675-470468 Fax.470871** A4097 > Kingsbury, 1m on R. Privately owned *** Hotel with 49 spacious en suite bedrooms. Excellent restaurant and bar meals. Leisure club with swimming pool. 9 hole golf course. Full Conference and banqueting facilities. Rural location,ample parking, night porter.
Pub Grub	9		**The White Horse Tel.01675-470227** A4097 > Sutton Coldfield, 400 yds on R. Open all day, food.12am-10pm. A traditional eating house, family play area.
Relax	10		**Drayton Manor Park & Zoo Tel.01827-287979 Fax.288916** Follow the signs off the motorway. Family Theme Park. Open from 9am - 6pm. Rides start at 10.30am. including "Stand up Coaster"

FUEL	10	ESSO	**A & M Garages Tel.01872-892333** A5 > Nuneaton. OPEN 24 hrs. All fuels, car wash, shop with microwave and coffee machine.
Service Area	10		**Granada, Tamworth Services. Tel.01827-260120** Follow the signs off the motorway Restaurant, Burger King, shop, phones, Granada Lodge,
Pub Grub Restaurant	10		**Centurion Park Tel. 01827 260587** A5 > Tamworth 1st exit > Stonydelph on L. (1.5 m Off) Our delicious menu provides a wide selection of value for money meals, as well as our own "daily specials". We look forward to welcoming you. Baby changing facilities. Toddler area. Garden. Childrens Parties. Outdoor play equipment. Disabled facilities.
Restaurant	10		**A. J's. Family Restaurant.** A5 > Atherstone. 1m. on the L. Open from 7am. All facilities, Adult and children's menu available all day.
FUEL	11	FINA	**Fina Service Station** Follow the signs for the services Petrol station selling all fuels.
Take -away	11		**McDonald's** Follow the signs for the services Open 7am-11pm. Drive through and restaurant.

B&B	1		**Mrs Evans, B&B. Tel.01684-592013 Fax.592013** A38,> Worcester, follow >Ryall onL. (50yds.on bend) Old Farm House, Flexi Hours, TV & hot drinks in room
Cafe Diner	1		**Olde Hutte Cafe, Tel.01684-592384** A38 > Worcester,2nd Layby on L. (500 yds) OPEN 6.30-3.30.week days.(Sat 6-10.30am.) Good, Clean, Friendly, Cheap
REPAIRS	1	Q8	**Ryall Garage, Tel.01684-594624** A38 > Worcester, 1.5m on L. OPEN 8am-9pm. Vehicle Repairs, All Fuels, Friendly service,
CAMPING	2		**Kingsgreen Caravan Park, Tel.01531-650272** A417> Gloucester, 1st L.Malvern,(1m.) Open Mar-Nov.Tents & Vans, hook up,Fishing, Showers, Nr Malvern Hills.
B&B	3		**Linton Hall, Tel.01989-720276 Fax.720276** B4215> Gloucester, 0.7m. on R. Built 1888 in 8 acres, ETB 3 crown, All room en suite. Evening Meals.
Hotel	3		**Old Court Hotel, (3.6m.) Tel.01531-820522** B4221> Newent, close to centre of Newent,(old market town) Magnificent Manor House Hotel, en suite rooms, TV, Tea / Coffee etc., Superb restaurant and conference facilities. Secluded one acre walled gardens. Near to famous birds of prey centre, Shambles museum & 3 vineyards. Open all year. We look forward to seeing you.
Pub Grub	3		**Roadmaker Inn. Tel.01989-720352** >B4221 Newent, (0.3m.) Pub with bar food and Camping site

M50 Exit			*There is a 1000 year old Yew tree at Murch Marcle (north of Exit 4)*
Pub Grub	4		**Travellers Rest, Beefeater. Tel.01989-563861** On Exit roundabout Open 11am-11pm. (Food 12- 10.30) Families Welcome, Play area,
Service Area	4	(BP)	**Welcome Break, Ross Spur Services. Tel.01989-65301** A40 > Ross on Wye, 0n R. Granary self service restaurant, shop, baby change. B.P. fuels, water & air.

M53 Exit			*Port Sunlight, spectacular garden suburbs, late 19thC. Home of Sunlight Soap*
SUPER STORE FUEL	1	||||||| TESCO	**Tesco Super Store, Bidston Moss Tel.01516-510000** A554 > Birkenhead, 0.4m @ roundabout take 1st. exit. Petrol Station open 7am - 8.30pm. (Sun 9.30- 4.30) Facilities at this Super Store include:- Coffee Shop, Baby changing and toilets.
Pub Grub	3		**Arrow Park Hotel Tel.0151-677-5031** > Arrow Park Hospital, across roundabout Carpark on R. Open all day for food. Bar snacks & steaks 11.30-2.30. Function room,
REPAIRS	3		**Kwik-Fit Tel,0151-608-4821** > Birkenhead, 1m on l. Tyres. Exhausts. Shock absorbers. Brakes.
SUPER STORE	3		**J Sainsbury Plc. Tel.0151-608-9246** > Birkenhead, 0.75m on L. Open for fuel (Mon-Tues)7.30 am- 7,15 & Wed Thur Fri 7.30am-8.15pm.
Pub Grub	3		**Cherry Orchard Tel.0151-604-1241** > Arrow Park Hospital, L @ roundabout on R. Food served 11am-9pm. Full menu. Cask conditioned ales.
Pub Grub Restaurant	4	BREWERS FAYRE	**Acorn Hotel Tel. 01516 083216** >Birkenhead, 1m Turn R @ Traveller's Rest pub, Acorn is at bottom of of Village Rd. Our delicious menu provides a wide selection of value for money meals, as well as our own "daily specials". We look forward to welcoming you. Baby changing facilities. Garden. Childrens Parties. Disabled facilities. SPECIAL OFFER
Relax	4		**Country Mouse Tel.01513-425382** A5137 > Heswall, 1.25m on L. Craft Shop, Licensed restaurant serving coffee, lunches & teas.
FUEL	4	Mobil	**Spital Service Station Tel.0151-344-7504** > Bebington, 1m on R Open 7-10, (9-5 on Sun). Jet wash. Shop,
FUEL	4	Shell	**Drayton Motors Tel.01513-348602** > Clatter-bridge, 0.5m on R Open Mon-Fri 7am-8pm, Sat-Sun 8am-6pm. Full garage facilities.
Hotel	5		**Chimneys Hotel Tel.01513-273505** A550 > Queensferry, 0.5m L @ lights & L again into car park. Open for food 12-2,30 & 7-9. Rooms ensuite, drinks & TV. Lounge bar.
			Please remember to mention "Just Off..." when you visit one of our locations

Pub Grub Restaurant	5		**Burleydam Tel. 01513-398101** 
			A41 > Chester (1 m Off)
			Our delicious menu provides a wide selection of value for money meals, as well as our own 'daily specials'. We look forward to welcoming you. Baby changing facilities. Toddler area. Garden. Outdoor Play area. Fun Factory. Disabled facilities. Children's Parties. Accommodation. Breakfasts
Pub Grub	7		**The Foxfields Tel.01513-550200**
			> Whitby, 300yds on L.
			Open all day, Food served 11.30-2.30 & 6-9 on Thur Fri Sat. Beer Patio
FUEL	7	**ESSO**	**Overpool Service Station Tel.01513-551533**
			> Whitby, 0.5m across roundabout.
			OPEN 24 hours, Microwave snacks and hot drink machine. All Fuels.
Cafe Diner	8		**Carol's Kitchen Tel.01513-552137**
			> Portside North & South, 0.5m on R.
			Open 7.30-3pm Wide range of hot & cold food & drinks.
Take-away	8		**Rossmore Fish & Chips**
			> Rossmore Trading Estate, across roundabout, 1st R. (one way st.)
			Open 11.30-1.30 & 4.30-7pm for Fish & Chips & Chinese.
FUEL	8		**Hughes Service Station Tel.01513-273424**
			A550 > Queensferry, 0.75m on R.
			OPEN 24hours. All Fuels, Shop with Microwave snacks & Coffee.
REPAIRS	8		**J.M.C. Services (U.K.) Ltd.. Tel.01513-565566 Fax.569422**
			> Rossmore Trading Estate, > L. opposite Ford dealer.
			Open 8.30-5.30 (Sat 8.30-1) 24 hour recovery, Full workshop, Tyres,
FUEL	9	**Gulf**	**Telegraph Service Station Tel.01513-551710**
			> Town centre, 100 yds on L.
			OPEN 24 hours, All fuels, Car and Jet wash, Microwave in shop.
Relax	9		**The Boat Museum Tel.01513-555017 Fax.554079**
			Follow the signs from the motorway.
			Canal boats in & out of water, 60 boats to see. Cafe & boat trips.
B&B	9		**Fern Villa Tel.01513-554595**
			> Town Centre, 1st R. after garage.
			Basins in all rooms,Sat.TV, Hot drinks, Full breakfast, opt. eve. meal
Cafe Diner	10		**Rock Island Cafe Tel.01513-550965**
			> Mill Lane Ind. Estate
			Open 7-6.30 (Sat & Sun 7-1.30) Hot & cold food good choice for lunch,
CAMPING	10		**Chester Fairparks Caravan Club, Tel.01513-551600**
			Follow brown signs from the motorway roundabout.
			Open Apr - Oct. Very near Chester, hookups, shower & toilet block.
SUPER STORE	10		**J.Sainsbury Plc. Tel.01513-573181**
			> Queensferry, R @ next roundabout, >Town Centre,double back @ roundabout.
			Open for discount petrol.
Pub Grub Restaurant	12		**Wheatsheaf Tel. 01244-371159**
			A56 > Chester, A41 > Birkenhead, L @ lights (Heath Rd.) 500 yds on L (2.5m Off). Our delicious menu provides a wide selection of value for money meals, as well as our own "daily specials". We look forward to welcoming you. Baby changing facilities. Garden. Childrens Parties. Disabled facilities, Outdoor Play equipment.

Hotel	**12**		**Hoole Hall Hotel Tel.01244-350011** A56 > Chester, on the L. Fine hotel in beautiful 18th C. building, ideal business or pleasure.
Hotel	**12**	TOBY RESTAURANTS	**Royal Oak Hotel. Tel.01244-301391 Fax.301948** > Mickle Trafford, 200yds on R. RAC ***, 36 ensuite rooms. Toby restaurant, meeting rooms, 2 bars.

Hotel	**1**		**Featherstone Farm Hotel & King's Repose Restaurant, Tel.01902-725371** A460> Cannock. > L @ lights, 400 yards on R. A small high class hotel in 5 acres of unspoilt countrysise. 8 bedrooms, all en-suite and usual facilities. Self-contained cottages with service available. The King's Repose Restaurant is a meticulously converted medieval barn and we are very proud of our top class menus. Secure parking. SPECIAL OFFER
Pub Grub	**2**		**The Mortan Arms Tel.01902-787178** A449 Wolverhampton, L. @ lights, on R. Open 11.30-2.30 & 5-11. Full menu & specials at lunch time.
Cafe Diner	**3**		**Paulette Cabin Tel.01902-374679** Follow the signs for museum, > R just before railway bridge. Open 7.30 am-3.30pm Mon-Fri. Hot & cold food & drinks, ice creams, cigarettes.
Pub Grub	**3**		**The Bell Inn Tel.01952-850210** A41 > Whitchurch, 1m on L before petrol station. Open 11-3 & 5.30-11. Traditional Pub, families welcome, bar snacks & full menu.
Relax	**3**		**The Aerospace Museum Tel.01902-374112** Follow the signs from the Exit. Open 10-5. Royal Air Force Museum, 25 acres of aircraft,rocketry & aero engines.
FUEL	**3**	Shell	**Tong Self Service. Tel.01952-850260** A41 > Shifnal, 1m on L. Open 7am-10pm.Sat 8-10,Sun9-10. All fuels, shop with microwave & coffee machine
Take -away	**4**		**The Butty Box Tel.0374-720405** > Kidderminster, 300 yds. in layby on L. Mobile open 6.30-2.30 Mon-Fri, 6.30-11 Sat. Good hot food & drinks,toilet & tel
Cafe Diner	**6**		**McDonald's Tel.01952-260278** > Wellington, 200 yds. on L. Open 7.30am-11pm. Full McDonald's menu.
SUPER STORE **FUEL**	**6**	TESCO	**Tesco Super Store, Telford Tel.01952-223388** > Wellington, 300 yds on L. Petrol Station open 6am-midnight, Facilities at this Super Store include:- Coffee Shop. Dispensing Pharmacy, Baby changing and toilets.
Pub Grub Restaurant	**7**	BREWERS FAYRE	**Horseshoe Inn Tel. 01952 740238** B5061 (the old A5) > Shrewsbury, on L. (3.5 m Off) Our delicious menu provides a wide delection of value for money meals, as well as our own "daily specials". We look forward to welcoming you. Baby changing facilities.Toddler area. Garden. Childrens Parties. Outdoor play equipment. Disabled facilities. SPECIAL OFFER

FUEL	1	**ESSO**	**Broughton Service Station Tel.01772-863604** A6 > Garstang, 1m on R at lights. Open 7am-10pm 7days / week, Shop all fuels and microwave snacks.
Pub Grub Restaurant	1	BREWERS FAYRE	**Boars Head Hotel Tel. 01772-864330** A6 > Lancaster (2 m. Off) Our delicious menu provides a wide selection of value for money meals, as well as our own "daily specials". We look forward to welcoming you. Baby changing facilities. Garden. Disabled facilities.
Hotel	1		**Broughton Park Hotel & Country Club Tel.01772-864087 Fax. 861728** A6 > Garstang, 0.5m on R. ****Hotel, in very fine gardens,leisure club. AA 2 rosette Restaurant
Pub Grub	1		**Golden Ball Tel.01772-862746** A6 > Garstang 1m. on L. @ lights. Open 11-3 & 6-11. All day Sat & Sun.Traditional food house. Real ale.
Restaurant	3		**Ashina Indian Restaurant Tel.01253-836883** > Fleetwood, 0.5m on R. Full Indian menu & some English dishes, Licensed, & Take away.
Pub Grub	3		**The Blue Anchor Tel.01253-836283** > Fleetwood, 0.5m on R. Family Pub with Carvery. Large garden play area.
cAMPINg	4		**Under Hill Farm Camp Site Tel.01253-763107** 1st L. A583 > Kirkham, Through lights, site 1st on R. Caravan & Camp Site, hook-ups, washroom, toilets, showers & laundry. Dogs on lead.
Pub Grub Restaurant	4	BREWERS FAYRE	**Yeadon Way Tel. 01253-341415** > Blackpool South Shore. Pub is before 1st r'bout. (.5 m Off) Our delicious menu provides a wide selection of value for money meals, as well as our own "daily specials". We look forward to welcoming you. Baby changing facilities.Toddler area. Fun Factory. Garden. Childrens Parties. Outdoor play equipment. Disabled facilities. Accommodation. Breakfasts.
FUEL	4		**Elf Service Station Tel.01253-791416** A583 > Blackpool on R. Open 7am.-11pm. 7days, Shop, microwave snacks. Car wash.
SUPER STORE **FUEL**	4	TESCO	**Tesco Super Store, Blackpool Tel.01253-791503** A583 > Blackpool, 1st L 300 yds. Petrol Station open 8.30 am-8pm. (Sun 9.30 am- 4pm.) Facilities at this Super Store include:- Coffee Shop. Cash dispenser. Baby changing and toilets.
			Please remember to mention "Just Off..." **when you visit one of our locations**

	Exit		
SUPER STORE **FUEL**	**3**	IIIIIIIIII TESCO	**Tesco Super Store, Baguley Tel.01619-460988** A560 > Altrincham, into Altrincham Rd. Petrol Station OPEN 24 hours. Facilities at this Super Store include:- Coffee Shop. Cash dispenser. Baby changing and toilets.
Take-away	**6**		**Admiral's Fish & Chips.** A538 > Hale, park @ rear opposite the Unicorn, shop in the square Open Mon-Sat 11.30-2 & 4.15-9pm, Sun5-9pm.
Hotel	**6**		**The Unicorn Hotel Tel.01619-804347** A538 > Hale, 1.25 m on R. * Hotel with accommodation, full menu & Bar snacks, Food 12-2 & 6.30-9
FUEL	**6**		**Hale Barns Garage Tel.01619-804116** A538 > Hale, 1m. on R. Open 7am-8pm Weekdays, 8-5 Sat & 9-4 Sun. All fuels, small shop
Pub Grub	**6**		**Red Lion (Romper) Tel.0161-980-6806** A538. Wilmslow, 1st L. Open all day food served 12 - 2pm. Full menu & Bar snacks.
Hotel	**6**		**Four Seasons Hotel Tel.0161-904-0301 Fax.908-1787** > Hale, on the motorway roundabout. (5 mins Airport). Fine modern Hotel with Restaurant. Cocktail Bar. Business Centre etc.
Restaurant	**10**		**Halebarn's Tandori Tel.0161-904-9909** A538 > Hale, 1.25m on L. Open 5.30-11Mon-Thur, 4-12 Fri-Sat. Full Indian Menu, Licensed,
Pub Grub	**10**		**The Hollow Tree Tel.01925-730733** A49 > Whitchurch 50 yds on R. Large informal Family Dining Pub, with Funky Forrest & play area.
FUEL	**10**	**BURMAH**	**Red Ensign Tel.01244-880335** > Queensferry, 1m on L. OPEN 24 hrs, All Fuels, large shop with microwave snacks..
REPAIRS	**10**		**The Ring O' Bells Tel.01925-730551** A559 > Northwich Full garage facilities, workshop, recovery and all fuels.
Pub Grub	**10**		**The Ring O' Bells Tel.01925-730556** A559 > Northwich, 0.25m on L. Parking @ rear. Small traditional pub. Outdoor Bowls. Local pies, good beer.V.friendly.
Cafe Diner	**10**		**Frank's (Open W/days 7am-4pm) Tel.Mobile 0831-220282** A49 > Whitchurch, 400yds in lay by on R. Mobile snack Bar serving food & drinks with tables & chairs.
Pub Grub *Restaurant*	**11**	BREWERS FAYRE	**Preston Brook Tel. 01928-716829** > Preston Brook, Pub is on R (.5 m Off) Our delicious menu provides a wide selection of value for money meals, as well as our own "daily specials". We look forward to welcoming you. Baby changing facilities. Fun Factory. Garden. Childrens Parties. Outdoor play equipment. Disabled facilities. Accommodation. Breakfasts.
			REMEMBER – Tiredness kills – TAKE A BREAK

	Exit		
Relax / Pub Grub	11		**Sutton Fields, Tel.01928-791001** > A56 Chester, after mini roundabout, 1st L.> S-Weaver,on L under bridge. Open Mon-Fri 10am-9pm, and Sat & Sun 9am-6pm. Golf Driving Range & putting green Family Attractions. crazy golf, cafe and licensed beer garden, Pet animals MORE THAN MEETS THE EYE.
Relax	11		**Small car park** A56 > Preston Brook 0.5m on R @ the bottom of the hill. A small car park on the banks of the Trent & Mersey Canal.
Hotel	11		**De Vere Lord Daresbury Hotel Tel.01925-267331 Fax.265615** A56 > Warrington, 150 yds on L. **** Fine Modern Hotel for business or pleasure. Two restaurants.
Relax	11		**Daresbury Fruit Farm Tel.01925-740448** A56 > Warrington, 600yds on R along lane, 1m from motorway. Pick your own Fruit, Strawberries,Raspberries, Apples, Pears & Plums.
Hotel	11		**The Red Lion Hotel Tel.01928-701174** A56 > Preston Brook, 0.5 m on L. Home cooked food served 12-2 &6-9. Families welcome.En suite rooms TVetc
REPAIRS	12		**Sutton Weaver Service Station Tel.01928-718922** > Frodsham, L @ the lights. Open 8.30-6 & Sat morning. Full mechanical repairs. Recovery. MOT's.
Hotel	12		**Runcorn Forte Posthouse Tel.01928-714000 Fax.714611** A557 > Northwich, Follow the Hotel signs to the L. Spacious restaurant. Kids play area, Conference facilities.
FUEL	12	SPOT	**Sutton Weaver Service Station Tel.01928-718922** > Frodsham L @ the lights. OPEN 24 hours, All Fuels. Car wash. Large shop with microwave snacks.
Relax	14		**Picnic Area** Follow the signs from the motorway exit. Large car park with toilets and picnic area.
Relax	14		**Sail Sports, (Wind Surfing Centre) Tel.01928-740243** > Helsby, then follow the brown signs, 4m from exit. Windsurfers for hire. Male & female changing rooms, 40 acres.
Take -away	14		**G.K.Catering Tel.01514-235844** Follow the signs for the picnic area. OPEN 24 hrs, Mobile serving Burgers, Cakes, papers, cigarettes etc
FUEL	14	Shell	**Elton Green Service Station. Tel.01928-725144** A 5117 > Stanlow Open 7.30-6, & 9-4 w/ends. Workshops MOT's Shop with micro.
Pub Grub	14		**Helsby Arms Tel.01928-722165** A 56 > Helsby, 1m on the L. Open all day for drinks, food & coffee.
Pub Grub / Restaurant	16		**Wheatsheaf Tel. 01244-851804** A540 > Chester, 1mile. Our delicious menu provides a wide selection of value for money meals, as well as our own "daily specials". We look forward to welcoming you. Baby changing facilities. Play Zone. Garden. Childrens Parties. Outdoor play equipment. Disabled facilities.

M56 Exit

FUEL	16	Gulf	**Dunkirk Service Station Tel.01244-851631** > Whitchurch, R @ roundabout 400 yds on R. OPEN 24 hrs. All fuels, Jet wash, food, drinks & toilet.
Restaurant	16	LITTLE CHEF	**Little Chef Tel.01244-880132** > Queensferry, 1m. on L. Open 7am-10pm, Licensed, baby change & disabled facilities, Coffee stop. Fuel.
Cafe Diner	16		**Dunkirk Transport Cafe. Tel.01244-851655** > Whitchurch, 400 yds on R. OPEN 24 hrs.Selection of cooked food always available, Night parking

M57 Exit

Relax	2		**Knowsley Safari Park Tel.0151-430-9009** Follow the signs from the motorway. 5 mile drive around the Safari Park. Reptile centre & Amusement Park.
FUEL	2	BP	**Brookbridge B.P. Service Station.** > Prescot, on the junction roundabout. All fuels plus small shop.
Pub Grub	2		**The Clock Face Tel.0151-430-701** > Prescot 0.5 m on L, Open all day. Lunch time food. Families welcome. Beer Garden.
Pub Grub	2		**Hillside Hotel Tel.01514-891361** A57 > Liverpool, on R. @ roundabout. Open all day, for food and drinks, families welcome.
FUEL	6	Shell	**Shell Service Station Tel.0151-530-1764** > Fazakerly, 0.5m double back, garage on L OPEN 24 hrs. All fuels. Microwave & coffee machine.
FUEL	6	Mobil	**Clock House Service Station Tel.0151-525-6377** > Fazakerley, L @ Copplehouse Pub, 50yds on R. Open 7.30am -10pm, All fuels. Garage, workshop etc.
Pub Grub Restaurant	7	BREWERS FAYRE	**Punchbowl Tel. 01515-261018** *SPECIAL OFFER* A5036 > Bootle,R @ lights B5207> Thornton, R @ next lights, beside Sefton Church. Our delicious menu provides a wide selection of value for money meals, as well as our own 'daily specials'. We look forward to welcoming you. Baby changing facilities.Toddler area. Play Zone. Garden. Childrens Parties. Outdoor play equipment. Disabled facilities.
Restaurant	7	LITTLE CHEF	**Little Chef Tel.0151-526-2289** > Ormskirk, 0.25 m 0n L. Open 7am-10pm, Full Little Chef menu, Adjacent to Fuel.
SUPER STORE	7		**Asda** > Aintree Race Course, 300yds on L. Open 7am-10pm. All fuels. Jet wash,
Pub Grub	7		**Old Roan Tut'N'Shive Tel.0151-526-8422** > Aintree Race Course, 1.5m on R @ lights. Theme fun pub. Full menu served 12am -3pm. Open 11am -11pm.

Pub Grub	**3**	**Stanley Gate, Miller's Kitchen Tel.01695-27700** A 570 > Ormskirk. Open all day. Very varied menu. Beer garden & play area.
Take away	**3**	**Travel Chef Tel.01704-895294** A570 > St.Helens, 1m on L. in layby, Mobile Snack Bar.Open 7.30- 2pm Mon - Fri. Hot & cold food & drinks.
FUEL	**3** BURMAH	**4 Lane Ends Service Station Tel.01695-50346** > Southport, on next roundabout. OPEN 24 hrs. Shop. Car wash.
Restaurant	**3**	**Little Chef Tel.01695-50481** > Ormskirk, 200yds on R. Open 7am-10pm. Licensed. disabled and baby changing facilities. Fuel.

B&B	**4**	**The Flag Tel.0161-799-1200** A6 > Walkden, 0.75 m 0n L. TV in rooms, new extension with lounge. Full cooked breakfast.
Pub Grub	**4**	**The Red Lion Tel.01204-63257** A6 > Atherton, 1.5m on R. Steak house. Bar snacks available. Kids welcome. Country style pub.
Pub Grub	**4**	**Watergate Toll, Free House. Tel.01204-64989** A6 > Atherton 50 yds 0n R. Quality foods available all day, Cask conditioned beers.
Relax Restaurant	**5**	**Barton Grange Garden Centre Tel.01204-660660** A58 > Bolton, 0.5m on L. Open 9am-5.30pm. Sun. 10-5.30. Award winning Garden Centre. Offering a wide range of quality products for gardening and outdoor leisure. Attractive houseplant Department. Gift shop. Pets & Aquaticse. Hungry Gardener Restaurant open 10am-5pm. Home made food served daily.
Pub Grub	**5**	**The Three Pigeons Tel,01204-61678** A58 > Bolton on L. Steakhouse with full menu & cask conditioned beers.Open 12-3 & 5.30-11
Hotel	**5**	**Broomfield Hotel. Tel.01204-61570** A58 > Bolton 2m on R. * Hotel, En suite rooms with TV & Hot drinks.Full breakfast. Licensed.
Pub Grub Restaurant	**6**	**Royal Oak Tel. 01942-812168** A6 > Westhoughton. (.5 m Off.) Our delicious menu provides a wide selection of value for money meals, as well as our own "daily specials". We look forward to welcoming you. Baby changing facilities. Outdoor play equipment. Disabled facilities.
Hotel	**6**	**The Georgian House Hotel Tel.01942-814598** A6 > Chorley, 1.5m on R. ****Hotel, excellent leisure & Business facilities, indoor pool.
		Please remember to mention "Just Off..." **when you visit one of our locations**

Pub Grub	6		**The Royal Oak Tel.01942-812168** A6 > Wigan 300 yds on L. Parking @ rear. Open all day, Food 11.30-10pm. Full Menu, Families welcome.
SUPER STORE FUEL	6	TESCO	**Tesco Super Store, Horwich Tel.01942-692621** A6027 > Bolton, L @ lights, 200 yds on R. Petrol Station open 8am-8.30 pm. (Fri 8-9.30). Facilities at this Super Store include:- Restaurant, Home & Wear. Cash dispenser. Baby changing and toilets.
Service Area	S	BP	**Pavilion. Rivington Services. Tel.01204-68641** Follow the signs off the motorway. Barclays, Restaurant Cafe Games.BP.
Pub Grub Restaurant	8	BREWERS FAYRE	**Railway Hotel Tel. 01257-279410** Follow signs to Botany Bay. (1.7 m Off) Our delicious menu provides a wide selection of value for money meals, as well as our own "daily specials". We look forward to welcoming you. Garden. Childrens Parties. SPECIAL OFFER
Hotel	8		**Shaw Hill Hotel Golf & Country Club. Tel.01257-269221 Fax.261223** A6 > Leyland, 1.5m on L. A taste of classical elegance. 18 hole course, Superb Hotel.
FUEL	8	TEXACO	**Jubilee Service Station. Tel.01257-270688** A6 > Leyland, 1m on L. Open 7-10 Mon-Fri. All Fuels, Jet Wash, small shop.
Pub Grub	8		**The Hartwood Tel.01257-269966 Fax.241678** A6 > Chorley, Double back @ 2nd roundabout, 100yds on L. Ideal for business or pleasure, Food 11.30-10.30, All rooms en suite.
Hotel	8		**Parkville Country House Hotel Restaurant. Tel.01257-261881 Fa. 273171** A6 > Leyland, 1.5m on R. Ideal for business or pleasure, Fine restaurant, conference facilities.

Hotel	5		**The Derby Lodge Hotel Tel.0151-480-440 Fax. 480-8132** A5080. Huyton, 600 yds on R. Fine Country House Hotel. Bar & restaurant, Ideal business or pleasure
Relax	5		**The Golf Course Tel.0151-480-1901** > Huyton, 500 yds on L. Open to non members. Golf course with shop, tea & coffee & snacks.
Pub Grub	5		**The Stanley Arms Tel.0151-489-1747** > Huyton, 1m on L. Open all day, 11.30am-11pm, Full menu with steaks etc, Kids welcome.
Pub Grub Restaurant	6	BREWERS FAYRE	**Chapel Brook Tel. 01514-809614** A5080 > Huyton 1st R. (300yds Off) Our delicious menu provides a wide selection of value for money meals, as well as our own "daily specials". We look forward to welcoming you. Baby changing facilities.Toddler area. Fun Factory. Garden. Childrens Parties. Outdoor play equipment. Disabled facilities. Accommodation. Breakfasts. SPECIAL OFFER

Relax	6		**Knowsley Safari Park Tel.0151-430-9009** Take the M 57 and turn off @ Exit 2, follow the signs. 5 mile drive around the Safari Park, Reptile centre & Amusement Park.
Pub Grub Restaurant	7		**Micklehead Green Tel. 01744-818971** A570 > St. Helens. (1m Off). Our delicious menu provides a wide selection of value for money meals, as well as our own "daily specials". We look forward to welcoming you. Toddler area. Play Zone. Childrens Parties. Outdoor play equipment. Disabled facilities.
FUEL	7	Shell	**Rainhill Motors, Stoops Garage Tel.0151-426-4199** > Rainhill, 400yds on L. OPEN 24hrs. All fuels. Garage repair facilities & Servicing.
Pub Grub	7		**Ship Inn Tel.01514-264165** > Rainhill 0.75 m on L. Open for food, coffee & drinks from 11.30 -10.30pm.Families welcome.
Pub Grub	7		**Victoria Tel.01514-263694** > Rainhill, 1m on R. in village. Open all day. Food at lunch time. Disco in evenings.
Take-away	7		**Captain's Table Tel.01514-309655** > Rainhill, 1m on R. in village. Open 11.30-2 & 4.30-12. for FISH & CHIPS. Kebabs etc.
Service Area	S	Shell	**Welcome Break, Burtonwood Services. Tel.01925-51656** Follow the signs off the motorway Granary self service restaurant, Little Chef and Travel Lodge, baby change and disabled facilities. shop, phones, games, and toilets. Shell fuels, water & air.
Pub Grub	9		**The Swan Tavern Tel.01925-631416** A49 > Newton Willows 500yds on R. Open all day for food, coffee and drinks.Beer garden and good parking.
Pub Grub Restaurant	9		**Winwick Quay Tel. 01925 414417** A49 > Warrington (200 yds Off) Our delicious menu provides a wide selection of value for money meals, as well as our own "daily specials". We look forward to welcoming you. Baby changing facilities.Toddler area. Garden. Outdoor play equipment. Disabled facilities. Accommodation. Breakfasts.
FUEL	9	TEXACO	**Winwick,Texaco Service Station Tel.01925-638240** A49 > Warrington, 0.5m on L. Open 6am-10pm daily. All fuels. Car wash. Jet wash. Shop.
Service Area	S	**ESSO**	**Granada, Birch Services. Tel.01616-430911** Follow the signs Restaurant, Burger King, shop, phones, Granada Lodge,
Pub Grub	19		**The Duke of Wellington Tel.01763-60942** A6046 > Heywood, across roundabout, 1.5m on left. Open all day for coffee & drinks, weekday lunches, traditional town pub.
Restaurant	19		**Piccolo's Tel. 01706-365561** A6046, > Heywood, across roundabout, R @ junction, 1.5m on R. Open evenings, (closed Mon.) Licensed Italian Restaurant.

FUEL	**19**	TEXACO	**Hopwood Service Station Tel.01706-360557** A6046 > Heywood, 0.25m on L. OPEN 24 hours, Car wash & Large shop.
FUEL	**19**	Mobil	**Hollin Filling Station Tel.0161-6530709** A6046 > Middleton, 1m on L. Open 7am-11pm.Mon-Sat, 8am-11pm Sun. & Bank Holidays.
Pub Grub **Restaurant**	**21**	BREWERS FAYRE	**John Milne Tel. 01706-299999** — SPECIAL OFFER A663 > Shaw 1st on L, Pub is on left. Our delicious menu provides a wide selection of value for money meals, as well as our own "daily specials". We look forward to welcoming you. Baby changing facilities. Garden. Childrens Parties. Outdoor play equipment. Disabled facilities. Accommodation. Breakfasts.
Take-away	**21**		**New Hey Tel.01706-846941** A640 > Shaw, 1m on L. FISH & CHIPS or Chinese Open 11.30- 1.30, 5-11 (not Mon) You may ring
FUEL	**21**	Mobil	**Milnrow Service Station. Tel.01706-41132** A640 > Shaw, 1st L > Milnrow 0.5m on L. Open 6.30am-10pm (Sun 7-10) Jet Wash, All Fuels, Shop.
Pub Grub	**22**		**Juncton Inn Tel.01457-874265** A672 > Saddleworth, 2.25m on R. Open all day, every day,Breakfast, lunches, ev.meals,& coffee all day.
Pub Grub	**22**		**The Rams Head Inn Tel.01457-874802 Fax. 820978** A672 > Saddleworth, 1m on R. 400 yr.old Inn.Sea Food Speciality, Superb Views.Open 10-3 & 5.30-11.
FUEL	**22**	Mobil	**Shaw Petroleum Tel.01484-451362** A619 > Huddersfield, 0.5m on L. OPEN 24 hours, All Fuels, Car wash, Large shop, Microwave & drinks.
Pub Grub	**24**		**The Nags Head Tel.01422-373758** > Brighouse 2nd L @ roundabout 400yds on R. Open all day, Coffee, Food 12-2 & 6-9.30, Carvery & Bar meals.
Hotel	**24**		**Briar Court Hotel Tel.01484-519902 Fax.431812** A619 > Huddersfield, 0.5m on R. *** Hotel & Da Sandro Pizzeria. Lunches 12-2. Dinner 7-9.15..
Hotel	**24**		**Hilton National** A629 > Huddersfield, L @ roundabout, 50 yds. Another fine modern Hotel offering all facilities.
Pub Grub **Restaurant**	**25**	BREWERS FAYRE	**Armytage Arms Tel. 01484-712882** — SPECIAL OFFER A644 >Brighouse, R @ r'bout, pub is at top of hill on R (1.4 m Off) Our delicious menu provides a wide selection of value for money meals, as well as our own "daily specials". We look forward to welcoming you. Baby changing facilities.Toddler area. Garden. Childrens Parties. Outdoor play equipment. Disabled facilities.
Cafe Diner	**25**		**Shakys Tel.01422-311276** A644 > Brighouse, 500 yds double back, in Layby on L. Open 7.30am-5pm, All Day breakfast,Other foods & drink, Cake etc.,
Restaurant	**25**	LITTLE CHEF	**Little Chef Tel.01924-492329** A62 > Dewsbury, 200yds after lights on R. Open 7am-10pm. Licensed. disabled and baby changing facilities. Fuel.

Pub Grub	25		**The Corn Mill Hotel Tel.01484-400069** A644 > Dewsbury, 0.5 m on R. Open all day. Bistro Restaurant, Play area, Night club, Large car park
Hotel	25		**Forte Crest, Brighouse Tel.01484-400400 Fax. 400068** A644 > Brighouse, 800yds 1st R. 200yds on L. Fine modern hotel 24hr service, Pool, gym, saunas etc. Restaurant.
FUEL	25	**TOTAL**	**Service Garage Tel.01484-720371** A644 > Brighouse, 0.75 m on L. Open 7-9 Mon-Fri.(7-6 Sat, 9-6 Sun.) Shop with microwave, Car wash.
Service Area	S	**Shell**	**Welcome Break, Hartshead Moor Services. Tel.01274-876584** Follow the signs off the motorway Granary self service restaurant, Julie's Pantry, shop, card machine, games.
Pub Grub Restaurant	26	*(Brewers Fayre logo)*	**The Hunsworth Tel. 01274-862828** Adjacent to junction on the A58. Our delicious menu provides a wide selection of value for money meals, as well as our own "daily specials". We look forward to welcoming you. Baby changing facilities.Toddler area. Garden. Childrens Parties. Outdoor play equipment. Disabled facilities. Accommodation. Breakfasts. *(SPECIAL OFFER)*
SUPER STORE **FUEL**	26	IIIIIII TESCO	**Tesco Super Store, Cleckheaton Tel.01274-851331** A638 > Cleckheaton 0.9m turn R. > B6120 L into Northgate. Petrol Station open 8am - 8.30pm. (Sun 9.30- 4.30) Facilities at this Super Store include:- Baby changing toilets
FUEL	26		**Sunwin Service Station Tel.01274-677495** A58 > Halifax, 1m on R. Open 6-10, (Sun7-9) All fuels, Shop with microwave snacks, Car wash.
Take ~away	26		**Moorend Fishes** A638 > Dewsbury, 400yds on R. FISH & CHIPS Open 11.30-1.15 & Evenings (Closes 6pm Thurs.)
Cafe Diner	28		**The Red Brick Cafe Tel.01132-480667** A653 > Leeds, Double back on the roundabout, 200yds in layby. Open 7-3 Mon -Thur,(7-1.30 Fri,7-11 Sat). Hot & Cold food & drinks.
Pub Grub	28		**Beefeater Tel.01132-532768** A650 > Bradford on L. Open 11.30am -11pm. Food & Coffee all day, Families welcome.
FUEL	28	*JET*	**Woodmans Service Station Tel.01132-525997** A653 > Leeds, across roundabout, 1m from motorway. OPEN 24 hours, All fuels, Car wash, Shop. coffee & microwave snacks.
Pub Grub Restaurant	30	*(Brewers Fayre logo)*	**Oulton Lodge Tel. 01132-820202** A642 > York. (1 m Off) Our delicious menu provides a wide selection of value for money meals, as well as our own "daily specials". We look forward to welcoming you. Baby changing facilities.Toddler area. Garden. Childrens Parties. Outdoor play equipment. *(SPECIAL OFFER)*
REPAIRS	30		**Gordons Auto Centre Tel.01924-820266** A642 > Wakefield, 1m on L. Open 8,.30-6 (10-4 Sun). Tyres,exhausts, brakes & full workshop.

Hotel	30	TOBY RESTAURANTS	**The Grove Toby Hotel. Tel.01132-826201 Fax.829243** A642 > York, on R at the roundabout. Open to non residents, Bar & restaurant, Bedrooms ensuite.
Relax	30		**Rotherwell Sports Centre. Tel.01132-824110** A642 > York, 0.5m on R. 25 meter Swimming Pool, Squash courts, Bar & conference centre.
Pub Grub	31		**The Rising Sun Tel.01977-554766** A655 > Castleford, 0.5m on L. Open 11.30-2 & 7-11. Bar meals @ lunch time, families welcome.
Take ~away	31		**Whitewood Fisheries Tel.01977-519608** A655 > Castleford, 0.5m on R. opp the Rising Sun FISH & CHIPS.Open Mon-Sat 11.30-1.30, Thur 4.30-6.30, Fri 4.30-8.
B&B	31		**Whitewood Hall Guest House Tel.01977-517797** A655 > Castleford, 0.5m >L (@ pub) 400yds on L. 2 rooms ensuite, 1 family room. Full breakfast,TV & Hot drinks in rooms
Hotel	31		**The Village Tel.01924-897171** A655 > Normanton, 400 yds on L. 40 roomed Motel. Restaurant & Public Bar. ETB reg.Food 12-2 & 7-10pm.
FUEL	31	JET	**Prospect Garage Tel.01924-895840** A655 > Normanton, 1m on R. Open 6.45am-10pm (Sun8-10). All fuels. Jet wash.
Hotel	32		**The Parkside Inn Tel.01977-709911 Fax.701612** A628 > Pontefract, 500yds on L. Warm & friendly hotel with good conference facilities. Bar & restaurant.
FUEL	33	**BURMAH**	**Castleford Auto Point Tel.01977-553489** A639 > Castlleford, 0.5m on L. Open 6am-10pm (7 days) All Fuels, Large shop, microwave snacks.
FUEL	33	**Q8**	**Q8 Knottingley Tel.01977-673741** A645 > Knottingley, L & L again, 1m from motorway. OPEN 24 Hours. Car wash. Large shop with microwave snacks. All Fuels.
ꞦEPAIRS	33		**Motor City Tel.01977-670411** > Knottingly, 0.5m behind Q8 Fuel. Open 8.30-6 Mon-Sat (Sun10-2). Tyres, brakes, exhaust, batteries, MOT.
Service Area	33		**Granada, Ferrybridge Services. Tel.01977-672767** Follow the signs off the motorway. Restaurant, Burger King, shop, phones, lottery, card machine. Granada Lodge,
Restaurant	33		**Chestnut House Hotel Tel. 01977-600045** SPECIAL OFFER A1 >south. off @ 2nd slip Rd > Darrington, R >under bridge > L. (2.8m Off) The Chestnut House Hotel is ideally located for businessman & tourist alike. Offering a wide selection of restaurant & lounge meals & traditional beers This is a very comfortable,and friendly restaurant serving very good value meals, the carvery choice is excellent. Good parking. Easy access to A1.
Hotel	33		**Darrington Homespread & Hotel. Tel.01977-791458 Fax.602286** A1 > S.Doncaster, 2nd L, R @ bottom of slip road, under bridge, on L. Food served Noon-10pm. Kids indoor play area, All rooms en suite.
Pub Grub	34		**The George & Dragon Tel.01977-661319** A19 > Doncaster, 0.5m on R. Open 11.30-3 &5-11(Fri & Sat all day) Bar meals to restaurant standard.

REPAIRS	**34**		**Carroll Recovery Tel.01977-661256/661668** > Whitely 0.3m on R. Petrol, Accident & repairs.Collection & delivery.
Take-away	**34**		**Mobile Catering Tel.01757-228423** A19 > Selby 0.7m R > Goole, 1m on R Snack van selling Bacon & Burgers, Hot drinks Open 8-4 Mon-Fri.
Hotel	**36**		**Clifton Hotel Tel.01405-761336 Fax.762350** > Goole T.Centre, across 1st lights, R @ 2nd Lights 500 yds on L. Comfortable & Friendly ** Hotel. with full restaurant & Bar facilities
FUEL	**36**	**Shell**	**Glews Garage Tel.01405-764525** A614 > Bawtry, 300 yds on L. OPEN 24 Hours,all fuels, Country Kitchen Hot & Cold Food, car wash and vacuum
Pub Grub	**37**		**The Ferryboat Inn Tel.01430-430300** > Goole, L @ roundabout, 0.5m on L. Open for food 12-2 & 7-10pm, Bar snacks & full menu, Kids welcome.
FUEL	**37**	**Mobil**	**Brian Leighton Garages Ltd Tel.01430-432151** > Howden, R @ roundabout, 1m on R. OPEN 24 hours.All Fuels, Car wash, Large shop with microwave snacks.
Cafe Diner	**37**		**Nicky's Snack Bar. Tel.01405-767052** > Bridlington, 300yds on L. Open 7-3 Hot & Cold food & drinks. Tables & chairs. All day Breakfast.
FUEL	**37**	**RIX**	**J.Wardle & son Tel.01430-430388** > Goole, L @ roundabout, 200yds on R. Open 7.30am-10pm. All Fuels. Large shop with microwave,

Pub Grub **Restaurant**	**6**		**Mersey Farm Tel. 01619-628113** A6144 > Carrington Pub is on the L. (2 m Off) Our delicious menu provides a wide selection of value for money meals, as well as our own "daily specials". We look forward to welcoming you. Baby changing facilities.Toddler area. Play Zone. Childrens Parties. Outdoor play equipment. Disabled facilities. Accommodation. Breakfasts.	SPECIAL OFFER
Pub Grub **Restaurant**	**10**		**Cheadle Royal Tel. 01614-915884** On the Cheadle Royal r'bout beside to TGI Friday. Our delicious menu provides a wide selection of value for money meals, as well as our own "daily specials". We look forward to welcoming you. Baby changing facilities. Garden. Disabled Facilities. Accommodation. Breakfasts.	SPECIAL OFFER

**Please remember to mention "Just Off..."
when you visit one of our locations**

Take-away	6		**Rhodes on Roads Tel.01772-682105** Follow signs to B&Q, in car park Mobile open 8am-4pm. Hot & cold food & drinks, rolls etc.
Hotel	7		**Maple Lodge Hotel. Tel.01254-301284** > Clitheroe, R @ lights, 800yds on L. Small, Private Hotel, en suite rooms with cable TV. good parking.
Pub Grub	7		**Hyndburn Bridge Tel.01254-884287** > Clitheroe, R @ lights, L @ next lights, 1.5m on L. Well furbished traditional pub, Food served 12-2,& all day Fri-Sat-Sun
Hotel	7		**Dunkenhalgh Hotel Tel.01254-398021 Fax.872230** A6185 > Clitheroe, L @ lights, 100yds onL. 700 yr.old country house hotel, set in 17acres of Lancashire parkland.
FUEL	8	**JET**	**Griffin Head Service Stn. Tel.01254-234445** A 56 > Manchester, R. A679 > Accrington 200yds 0n R. Open 7am-10pm. (8-3 Sundays). All Fuels.
FUEL	10	**SAVE**	**Save Burnley Tel.01282-839574** E. bound Burnley, Hapton. W. bound Hapton > 0.5m on L. Open 7am-11pm.Daily, All Fuels, Jet wash, Grocery, Snacks,Drinks etc.
Relax	10		**Gawthorpe Hall, National Trust Tel.01282-779511** > Padiham, 1.5m on R. Follow brown signs. An early 17th C. House, Open Apr-Oct, 1pm-4.15pm, Closed Mon & Fri.
Restaurant	10		**Little Chef & Travel Lodge Tel.01282-831383** E. bound Burnley, Coal Clough. W. bound Coal Clough. On left. Open 7am-10pm. baby change & disabled facilities, Travel Lodge.
Hotel	12		**Wintersfield Hotel Tel.01282-615379** > Nelson, L. @ roundabout 300 yds. Wide range of rooms available, continental breakfasts.
FUEL	12		**Hollin Bank Service Stn. Tel.01282-619110** > Nelson, on L. OPEN 24 hours. Bakery, Large shop & microwave snacks.
Take-away	12		**Hill's Chippy Tel.01282-612539** > Burnley, R @ 1st lights, down hill 100yds on R. Open 11.30-1 & 4.30-6 Mon-Fri.,(Closed Mon & Tues ev.)clean & friendly
Hotel	12		**The Groves Hotel. Tel.01282-615948** > Nelson, L @ roundabout, Hotel is on the L. A warm & friendly hotel with night club, LARGE breakfast.
FUEL	13		**Nelson Auto Point Tel.01282-697666** > Nelson town centre, L @ 1st lights, 400yds on R. OPEN 24 hrs. All fuels, Small shop selling gas, drinks and food.
REPAIRS	13		**Kwik Fit Tel.01282-693530** > Nelson town centre, L @ 1st Lights, 400yds on L. Open 7 days / week for Tyres, Exhausts, Batteries, Shock absorbers.
Pub Grub	13		**The George & Dragon. Tel.01282-612929** > Kendal, 0.75m on L. Open 12-3 & 5.30-11.Full menu & specials board. Coffee served all day.

REMEMBER – Tiredness kills – TAKE A BREAK

REPAIRS	14		**John MacAdam & Son Ltd. Tel.01282-863851** > Keighley, Through lights, 2nd L. off roundabout on L. Open 8-6 Mon-Fri (8-2 Sat) Accident repairs etc.(Recovery Tel.868653.)
Pub Grub Restaurant	14		**Langroyd Hall Tel. 01282-864024** A6068 > Skipton, L @ 2nd lights, .5m on L. Our delicious menu provides a wide selection of value for money meals, as well as our own 'daily specials'. We look forward to welcoming you. Baby changing facilities. Garden. Childrens Parties. Outdoor play equipment. Disabled facilities.

Pub Grub	2		**The Seven Stars Tel.01617647305** A58 > Bury, !50 yds on R. Parking at rear. Full menu & Specials. Open 12-3 & 5-11, Coffee.
FUEL	2	BP	**Motorway Service Stn. Tel.0161-764-1347** A58 > Bury, 300yds on R. OPEN 24 hrs. All Fuels. Car wash. Shop with microwave snacks.
Pub Grub	2		**The Old Boars Head Tel.01617-643507** A58 > Heywood, 200yds on L. Large car park. Open all day, Food 12 am-10 pm. Draught Bass, Families welcome.
FUEL	2	Shell	**Heap Bridge Filling Stn. Tel.0161-761-7211** A58 > Heywood, 400yds on R. OPEN 24 hours, Microwave snacks in shop. All Fuels. HGV lane.
SUPER STORE	3		**Asda Super Store** > Pilsworth Ind. Estate, 0.25m on L. Open 8am-10pm. (Mon,Tue,Sat, 8-8.30 & Sun 10-4) All Fuels
Relax	3		**Megabowl Tel.016-767-9150 Fax.767-9156** > Pilsworth Ind. Estate. 34 lane 10 pin Bowling Alley,Licensed Bar,Megabite diner,Open 7day/wK.
Restaurant	3		**Deep Pan Pizza Co. Tel.01617-679132** > Pilsworth Ind Estate. 0.25m American theme Pizza Bar with pastas & salads, Licensed.Open 12am-11pm
Restaurant	3		**Chiqurito Mexican Restaurant Tel.01796-2591** > Plisworth Ind. Estate Open 12am-11pm All week., Licensed Mexican Restaurant, Kids welcome.
Relax	3		**Warner Cinemas. Tel.01617-662440** > Pilsworth Ind. Estate Cinema, phone to find out whats on.

Please remember to mention "Just Off..."
when you visit one of our locations

	Exit		
Pub Grub	1		**The Hinckley Knight Tel.01455-610773** A5 > Nuneaton, 0.25m 0n R. Open 11am-11pm. for food, drinks coffee etc. Bar & restaurant. Families welcome.
FUEL	1	TEXACO	**Texaco Three Pots Service Station Tel.01455-250431** A5 > Nuneaton, 0.25m on R. OPEN 24 hrs. All fuels and microwave snacks.
Hotel	1		**Hinckley Island Hotel Tel.01455-631122 Fax.634536** A5 > London, 300yds on L. Refreshingly different fine Hotel. Superb accommodation, leisure facilities.
Restaurant	1		**Barnacles Tel.01455-633220 Fax.250861** A5 > London, 100 yds on R. Open 12.30-2pm & 7.30-10pm. (Closed Sun & Mon am.) Fish restaurant and shop.

	Exit		
cAMPiNg	5		**Strathclyde Country Park Tel.01698-266155** Signed on the roundabout Large open area, Caravans, Campers & Tents.Hook up. Showers,Bike Hire.
Relax	5		**Strathclyde Country Park Tel.01698-266155** Signed on the roundabout. Large Recreational Parkland with Lake (Sailing) Fun Fair and walks.
REPAIRS	5		**Autoglass Tel.01968-852674** A7071 > Hamilton, on roundabout 0.5m. Windscreen repair specialists.
Service Area	S	BP	**Road Chef, Bothwell services. S.Bound ONLY Tel.01698-854123** SOUTH BOUND ONLY, follow the signs BP fuel, Self service restaurant. Play area.
Service Area	S	BP	**Road Chef, Hamilton Services. N. Bound ONLY. Tel.01698-282176** NORTH BOUND ONLY, Follow the signs off the motorway. BP Road Chef restaurant and shop.
FUEL	6	JET	**Hamilton Service Station Tel.01698-281222** A723 > Motherwell, Through the lights, on L. (0,5m) OPEN 24 hrs. Small shop with Microwave snacks.
Hotel	8		**Shawlands Hotel Tel.01698-792001** A71 > Edinburgh, On the L. Private hotel & a la carte Restaurant, Ideal for Business or pleasure.
REPAIRS	8		**Thomson's Tyres & Exhaust. Tel.01698-888888** A71 > Newmains,(East) 1m to lights & on L. Open 9-6 Mon-Fri, (-4.30 Sat.) Full range of tyres & exhausts.
Service Area	14	TEXACO	**Annandale, Blue Boar Services. Tel.0800-741174** Follow the signs off the motorway. Texaco.
B&B	S 11/12		**Woodside, B&B Tel.01555-851469** On B7078. N.bound turn off @ Exit 12 / S.bound turn off @ Exit 11 1 double & 2 twin rooms. Lounge & TV. Bath rooms. Full breakfast.
			REMEMBER – Tiredness kills – TAKE A BREAK

	Exit		
Service Area	**S** 11/12	**Gulf**	**Cairn Lodge Service Area** Turn off N.bound at Exit 11, / S bound at Exit 12 Independent service area, different and very pleasant. Fine restaurant
Service Area	**13**	**Shell** / **LITTLE CHEF**	**Welcome Break, Abington Services. Tel.01864-502637** Follow the signs off the motorway Granary self service restaurant, shop, phones, games. Travel information. Little Chef and Travel Lodge, baby change and disabled facilities. Caravan Park. Shell fuels, water & air.
Hotel	**13**		**Abington Hotel Tel.01864-502467 Fax.502223** A702 > Abington, 0.75 m. in village. The hotel provides an ideal location. So peaceful yet so close to the motorway.
REPAIRS	**13**		**The Garage Tel.01864-502 375** A702 > Abington 0.5 m on L. Open 8-5 (9-2 Sat.) Full workshop. Repairs. Servicing. Tyres & Exhaust
B&B	**13**		**Kersdale, B&B Tel.01864-502323** A702 > Abington, 1m in village on L. Open March-end October. TV lounge. Parking.En-suite available.Scottish breakfast. Clyde Valley T.Board.
Cafe Diner	**14**		**The Heatherghyll Hotel Tel.01864-502641** >Crawford @ North end of village. Cafe. Bar. Accommodation. Repairs.
REPAIRS	**14**		**South Scotland Coachworks Tel.01864-502236 Fax. 502635** > Crawford in village 24 hour recovery, Body & mechanical repairs. Good stock of general spare parts.
Cafe Diner	**14**		**Merlindale Cafe Tel.01864-502630** > Crawford at the S. end of the village. Transport Cafe, meals from 6am-10pm (7days,) also B&B. Good parking.
CAMPING	**14**		**Crawford Caravan & Camp Site Tel.01864-502258** > Crawford, 1m in centre of village Hook up, Showers, Hot & Cold water, Toilets, Caravan club.
Relax	**14**		**Picnic Area** > Crawford, in the village turn off at the mamorial over the railway and river bridges and park up in peace for a picnic, see the ruined castle in the trees.
Hotel	**17**		**The Dryfesdale Hotel Tel.01576-202427 Fax.204187** B7068 > Lockerbie, L @ roundabout, on the L. 4 Crown highly commended Hotel with restaurant. (Business meetings speciality).
Hotel	**17**		**Lockerbie Manor Country Hotel Tel.01576-202010 Fax.203046** > Lockerbie, sign posted after roundabout. Fine Georgian Mansion in 78 acres. 30 en suite bedrooms each one unique.
CAMPING	**17**		**Lockerbie Camp site.** > Lockerbie, into village, turn R. @ T-junction on to Glasgow Road, Camp site on R beside squash courts and ice rink.
B&B	**22**		**Craigarran Tel.01461-337768** A6071 > Springfield on R. Open all year for B&B. Full Breakfast.
Relax	**22**		**Gretna Museum & Tourist Services Ltd. Tel.01461-338441** Follow the Tourist Board Signs. Famous Old Blacksmith's Shop. Tartan & Tweed shop. Restaurant. Art Centre.

Take-away	22		**Solway Pizzaria Tel.01461-337234** A6071 > Gretna, 1st L @ post office, on L. Wide range of Pizzas and Kebabs to take away.

REPAIRS	4		**M & J Tyres Tel.01324-840235** > Falkirk, > R 0.75m. on L beside bed centre. In trade centre. Tyres. Engine tuning.
Service Area	9		**Granada, Stirling Services. Tel.01786-813614** Follow the signs off the motorway Country kitchen Restaurant, Burger King, shop, Information, Granada Lodge

FUEL	1	Shell	**Shell Camdean Tel.01383-418398** > Kincardine, on the L. OPEN 24 hrs, Shell Select Shop with microwave snacks. Car wash. HGV lane.
Hotel	1		**Queensferry Lodge Hotel Tel.01383-410000 Fax.419708** > Inverkeithing, R @ roundabout and follow the signs. A fine modern Hotel with dramatic views. Ideal business or pleasure.
Relax	1		**Deep Sea World Tel.01383-411411 Fax.410514** Follow the signs to Deep Sea World Fantastic ! Well worth a visit, of interest to the whole family.
Relax	1		**Forth bridge Viewing Area & Information** > Inverkeithing, R @ roundabout and follow the signs. Tourist information beside the Hotel, open 10am-6pm.
Pub Grub Restaurant	3	BREWERS FAYRE	**Halbeath Park Tel. 01383-620737** A907 > Dunfermline .5m on R. Our delicious menu provides a wide selection of value for money meals, as well as our own "daily specials". We look forward to welcoming you. Baby changing facilities. Toddler area. Garden. Childrens Parties. Outdoor play equipment. Disabled facilities.
Take-away	3		**Armando's Fish & Chips** A907 > Dunfermline, Open 11.30am-2pm, & 4.30pm- midnight, Closed Monday.
FUEL	3	BP	**Octopus Petrolium Tel.01383-722187** A907 > Dunfermline, 0.5m on R. Open 7am-10pm, All fuels, shop with microsnacks.
SUPER STORE	3		**ASDA** A907 > Dunfirmline, through roundabout on R Open 7.30am-8pm (Sun10-6) Jet wash. Discount fuel. Lottery
REPAIRS	4		**F & J Motors Tel.01383-831816 Fax.839633** A909 > Kelty, through village on R. Open 8-7 (9-5 On Sat & Sun) Petrol. All repairs. Tyres & Exhausts.

REMEMBER – Tiredness kills – TAKE A BREAK

Category	Exit	Brand	Details
Restaurant	4		**The Butterchurn Restaurant & Craft Shop Tel.01383-830169** B914 > Dollar, 100yds on L. Delicious homemade food served all day, Home baking and preserves for sale to take away. Pets corner and play area for children. Open every day 10 am-5.30pm. Fri. Sat. Sun. Last orders 8.30 pm. Closed Dec 25th to beginning of February.
Relax	6		**Findlay Clark Garden Centre Tel.01577-863327** A977. > Kincardine Bridge 150 yds on R. Garden centre.Indoor & out door coffee shop. Craft centre. Golf Shop.
Relax	6		**The Scottish Centre for Falconry Tel.01577-862010** A977 > Kincardine, 150yds on R. Open Apr - Sept. 10.30 am-5pm., Flying displays & audio visual theatre.
Relax	6		**Loch Leven Castle** A922 > Kinross, R in town centre & follow the signs. Free Lochside parking, Picnic area, toilets. Passenger ferry to Castle
Service Area	6	ESSO	**Granada, Kinross Services. Tel.01577-863123** Follow the signs Restaurant, Burger King, shop, phones, lottery. Camp site. Granada Lodge,
Hotel	6		**Croftbank Hotel Tel.01577-863819** > Kinross 0.5m opposite the school on L. Victorian House Hotel with Master Chef Patron, All rooms en suite.
Restaurant	6		**Heatheryford.Restaurant & Fishery Tel.01577-864212** A977 > Kincardine Bridge 100yds on L. Open 10-9pm. A la carte Restaurant. Accommodation and Trout Fishery.
Pub Grub	9		**The Baiglie Inn** A912 > Newburgh, 1.75m & R @ roundabout. Open 11am-2.30 & 5-11pm. for coffee, drinks and bar meals.
B&B	9		**Earnmhor, B&B. Tel.01738-812577** A912 > Bridge of Earn, 0.5m on R. Twin, double & 2 single rooms, TV & Drinks. Full Breakfast.
Relax	11		**Bell's Cherrybank Gardens Tel.01738-627330** > Perth 0.5m on R. Open 9-5 May -Oct. Outstandingly beautiful Heather Gardens and Cafe.
FUEL	11	SAVE	**Cherrybank Autopoint Tel.01738-628497** > Perth, 0.5m on R. Open 7am-11pm (7 days) All fuels, cold drinks and snacks.
Pub Grub	11		**Cherrybank Inn Tel.01738-624349** > Perth, 1m on R.Turn down slip road. Open all day, Food 12-2 &7-9. Full Bar menu. Accommodation.
CAMPING	11		**Cleeve Caravan Park, Tel.01738-639521** > Perth on the L. Caravans Tents & Campers. Shop. Laundry. Hookups. Play area.

Please remember to mention "Just Off..." when you visit one of our locations

The road crosses over the river Trent and vast areas of ancient fen land

Pub Grub	2		**The New Trent** A161 > Crowle over railway > R Ealand. Open 12-3 & 7-11.Hot & Cold food,Games room, Beer garden,good parking
Relax	2		**Severn Lakes Leisure Park Tel.01724-710245** A161 > Crowle, 2m on L. Camping, Caravaning, Motel, Restaurant, Water sports Centre.
Hotel	4		**Briggate Lodge Inn Tel.01652-650770 Fax.650495** A18 > Brigg, across roundabout and on the L. *** Hotel, ETB 5 Crown Highly commended, Ideal business or pleasure.
Cafe Diner	4		**Dot's Diner Tel.01652-657864** A18 >Brigg, 400yds on L. Open 6am-3.30pm (Sat 6-12.30) Portacabin clean & warm, Hot & Cold food.
FUEL	5	TEXACO	**Barnetby Service Stn. Tel.01652-688409** On the junction roundabout OPEN 24 hours. All Fuels Shop with microwave snacks.
Restaurant	5	LITTLE CHEF	**Little Chef Tel.01652-680798** On Roundabout Open 7am-10pm. Licensed, baby change & disabled facilities, Coffee stop. Fuel.

South lies the Antonine Wall, Roman, built to contain the Scots – it didn't work!

FUEL	3	Q8	**Q8 Kincardine Bridge Tel.01324-831006** On the roundabout OPEN 24 hours. All fuels. Shop. Cafe bar.
Pub Grub	3	BREWERS FAYRE	**Bowtrees Farm Tel. 01324-831125** On the roundabout Our delicious menu provides a wide selection of value for money meals, as well as our own "daily specials". We look forward to welcoming you. Baby changing facilities.Toddler area.Fun Factory. Garden. Childrens Parties. Outdoor play equipment. Disabled facilities.
FUEL	3	Shell	**Shell, Kincardine Bridge Tel.01324-831685** On the roundabout. OPEN 24 hrs. Shell Select Shop with microwave. Jet wash.

Ayot St Lawrence, home of George Bernard Shaw (west of Exit 6)

Relax	4		**Stanborough Park Tel.01707-327655 Fax.393281** Follow sign for town centre, around top roundabout & you will see it. Sailing,Windsurfing, Rowing, Walking, Fishing, Cafe & Nature Reserve.
SUPER STORE **FUEL**	4	TESCO	**Tesco Super Store, Hatfield Tel.01707-273314** > Hertford on R. Petrol Station OPEN 24 hours. Facilities at this Super Store include:- Coffee Shop. Dispensing Pharmacy, Cash dispenser. Baby changing and toilets.
Take -away	7		**Burger King Drive Through.** A602 > Stevenage across 1st roundabout, >L @ next roundabout & L again. Open 8am-11pm, (Sun 9-11) Full Burger King Menu.

A1M	Exit		Benington Lordship Gardens (E of Exit 7), rock, water, kitchen and rose gardens
Hotel	7		**Novotel Tel.01438-742299 Fax.723872** > Knebworth House, 200 yds on L, ***Hotel, Outdoor pool, Restaurant open to non residents.
Take -away	7		**Pizza Hut** A 602 > Stevenage, across 1st roundabout, L @ next roundabout, & L again. Open 12am-11pm 7days / week. Full range of Pizzas.
Relax	7		**Knebworth House Tel.01438-812661** > Follow signs for the house. Country House & 14 acres of Garden. Adventure play area. Open Apr-Oct.
SUPER STORE **FUEL**	7	IIIIIII TESCO	**Tesco Super Store, Stevenage Tel.01438-741399** A602 > Stevenage,0.5m. L. @ 2nd roundabout,- 1m. - L.@ 2nd roundabout again. Petrol Station open 6am. - midnight. Facilities at this Super Store include:- Coffee Shop. Dispensing Pharmacy, Baby changing and toilets.
Pub Grub	8		**George & Dragon Tel.01438-351362** B197 > Graveley 0.5 m on L. Open 11-3pm &5-11pm. Full, menu & bar snacks.
Relax Cafe Diner	8		**The Stevenage Garden Centre Ltd., Tel.01438-312660 Fax.314093** B197 > Graveley Rd. 300yds on R. Open 7 days, 9 am- 5.30 pm. Large Garden Centre with toilet facilities. Pleasant Tea / Coffee shop serving home made cake and pastries, home made soups, hot and cold drinks. Tropical and cold water fish and accessories. Large free car park.
Pub Grub	8		**The Wagon & Horse Tel.01438-367658** B197 > Graveley 0.5m on L. Open all day for food and drinks.Trad. village pub, good parking.
SUPER STORE	8		**J.Sainsbury Plc.** A602 > Stevenage, 300 yds on R. Open 6am-10pm (Sun 8-8) All Fuels, Cafe in Store.
Hotel	8		**Travel Inn Tel.01438-351318** A602 > Stevenage, 100yds on R. Reception 7am-11pm. All rooms ensuite with TV tea & Coffee etc.
Pub Grub	9		**The George IV. Tel.01462-892367** A6141 > Baldock, 1.5m on R. A pub for all ages, Hot & Cold food lunch time & evenings.
FUEL	9	Shell	**Shell, Letchworth. Tel;01462-473000** A6141 > Letchworth, 0.5m on L. Open 6.30 am- 10.30pm. Shell Select Shop with microwave snacks and car wash,
Service Area	34	**ESSO**	**Granada, Blyth Services. Tel.01909-591841** Follow the signs Restaurant, Burger King, shop, phones, Granada Lodge,
Pub Grub	36		**The Cecil Hotel Tel.01302-853123** A630 > Rotherham, 0.75m on L. Open all day. Good Food served from 12am- 2.30 & 6-9pm. Keen Prices. Traditional Pub Atmosphere Quizzes 4 nights per week, Pool, Snooker Darts. Children's play area.

A1M Exit			*The area of the Dukeries, many large estates once owned by the aristocracy (Exit 36)*
Pub Grub	36		**The Winning Post. Tel.01302-985349** A630 > Doncaster, 200 yds on L. Open Mon-Thur 12-3 & 7-11(Fri Sat All Day) Hot & Cold food & drinks.
Hotel	36		**The Moat House, Doncaster. Tel.01302-310331** A630 > Rotherham, 100yds on L. *** Hotel, leisure facilities, Bar,Restaurant, En suite rooms
FUEL	36	TEXACO	**Fallon, Doncaster** A630, > Conisbrough, 0.5m on R. OPEN 24 hours. All fuels, microwave snacks in shop.
Relax	37		**Museum of South Yorkshire Life Tel.01302-782342** A635 > Doncaster, Follow the brown signs to the R. Country house, Gardens, Tea room & Shop. Free Admission.
Pub Grub Restaurant	37		**Marr Lodge Tel.01302-390355 Fax.390357** A635 > Barnsley 0.7m on R. Open 8.30am-11pm. Breakfasts, Bar Snacks, Carvery, Families Welcome, Conference and meeting facilities are available.
Restaurant	M 62		**Chestnut House Hotel Tel. 01977-600045** A1 >south. off @ 2nd slip Rd > Darrington, R >under bridge > L. (2.8m Off) The Chestnut House Hotel is ideally located for businessman & tourist alike. Offering a wide selection of restaurant & lounge meals & traditional beers This is a very comfortable,and friendly restaurant serving very good value meals, the carvery choice is excellent. Good parking. Easy access to A1.	SPECIAL OFFER
Pub Grub Restaurant	62	BREWERS ESTATE	**Thinford Inn Tel. 01388-819394** A688 >Bishop Auckland. on junction with the A167. (3 m Off) Our delicious menu provides a wide selection of value for money meals, as well as our own "daily specials". We look forward to welcoming you. Baby changing facilities. Toddler area. Garden. Childrens Parties. Outdoor play equipment. Disabled facilities.	SPECIAL OFFER

The Old Schoolhouse
Spring 1997 Tariffs

B&B single £25, Double £40 / night. (Weekly self-catering.Double room £200 in season or £150 out of season.)
Situated on the southern outskirts of St Albans 5 mins walk from station and with excellent local facilities.
Each room has shower/WC, tea & Coffee, Fridge, microwave TV & central heating.

If you show us this book we will discount the above rates by 10% for one night or 20% for two or more nights for each member of your group.

16th Century Pub & Tea Rooms.

The Angel Inn (Free House), Toddington.
Past the village green, on the left, opposite the shops.
CAMRA Good beer Guide, Open All Day.
Trad Jazz every Sunday Lunch time.

On production of this book The Angel Inn will be pleased to serve FREE coffee or tea with every main course ordered.

Graham & Isla Lake welcome you to

The Coach House.

The Old Rectory, Marston Moretyne, Bedford, MK43 0NF.
Tel. 01234-767794
Situated in 5 acres of peaceful surroundings

Do not tear out.
Show us this book and we will give you a 10% Discount.
Each time you call.

The Bell is a Victorian village pub with large carpark and good facilities for children we have a non smoking Dinning area and serve light bites, grills, home made specials and coffee.
Coaches by appointment.

This is an ongoing offer. Do not tear out. Show us this book and we will give you a 10% Discount on all your meals each time you call.

Order a 2 course meal for each person and we will serve you your Tea or Coffee Free.

The Rose & Crown Inn,
Ridgmont.

Close to Woburn Abbey & Safari Park. Just off M1 Exit 13

This voucher entitles you to
£1 off
FISH & CHIPS
OR BREAKFAST
when presented at the restaurant or takeaway
One Voucher per Meal
Not to be used in conjuction with any other offer
NO CHANGE GIVEN

44 LONDON RD BAGSHOT SURREY
TEL 01276473193

Tear out this token and present it when ordering your main course and we will give you a glass of wine or soft drink for each adult main course ordered.
"Max 4 adults"

The Queen Inn, Dummer Village is an ancient building with many fine features.
We pride ourselves that the care and attention we offer our customers is worthy of the surroundings.
"We want you to feel welcome".

Present this coupon and we shall be pleased to discount our charges for one nights accommodation for each member of your party by 10%

Rainworth Guest House is a large spacious house with a peaceful & delightfully relaxed atmosphere. Guests can be assured of excellent accommodation, traditional comfort & warm hospitality.
Within the grounds, leisure facilities include a tennis court, but horse riding squash, golf & swimming can be arranged at local venues. Windsor Castle, Great Park & Racecourse are within easy reach.

This token entitles you to a free sweet if you order a starter & main course. This applies for each member of your party.

This offer expires on 1st January 2000.
It has been made by the business concerned.
The management of the "Just Off..."
disclaim any responsibility

The Pheasant Inn

Only 0.3m from the motorway with fine views over the fields.
Good food and bar snacks served between
12 - 2.30 & 6.30 - 9.30.pm
Families are welcome.
Coach parties by appointment

We want you to call at the WILDMOOR OAK time and time again, and every time you come we will give you a FREE glass of wine or soft drink with every main course you order from our menu card.
(This dose not include our blackboard specials).
We are justly proud of our home cooking and include Fish and Vegetarian dishes on our menu.

This offer expires on 1st January 2000.
It has been made by the business concerned.
The management of the "Just Off..."
disclaim any responsibility

THE WILDMOOR OAK

The Swan in Whittington,
Early Bird Discount.

Order your food between 12 noon - 1pm
or 6.15 -7.15pm, show us this book and we shall be
pleased to give you a 25% discount off your food
order. You may take advantage of this offer as
many times as you like whilst it is still valid.

This offer expires on 1st January 2000.
It has been made by the business concerned.
The management of the "Just Off..." disclaim any responsibility

The Swan
in Whittington

We advise you ring & book

This is an ongoing offer. Show us this book and We will give free Tea or Coffee to each member of your party who buys a meal or Bar snack.

This offer expires on 1st January 2000.
It has been made by the business concerned.
The management of the "Just Off..."
disclaim any responsibility

The George Inn

18th century pub and camp site with riverside location. There is an excellent children's corner with animals and we serve good food and ales all day.
OPEN 11am-11pm

Please present this token on arrival & we will discount the first night tariff for a double or single room by 10%. We advise you to ring ahead.

Priors Mead is a large Edwardian house set in beautiful grounds, off a quiet urban road. Guests can enjoy our swimming pool, croquet and baby grand piano. Walk to the town, play on championship golf course, or visit the beach.
An ideal touring base

The Weary Traveller

Choose two main courses and the least expensive is half price if you show us this advertisement.
This is an on going offer so don't detach the ticket. We want you to call again.
Thank You.

The Weary Traveller
Cullompton. Devon.

Please present this token at reception or in the restaurant and we shall be pleased to deduct 10%

Featherstone Farm Hotel and the King's Repose Restaurant are beautifully restored ancient buildings standing in 5 acres of unspoiled countryside.
Privately managed, the service, surroundings, menus and accommodation are all presented to the highest of standards and there is a walled car park with security lighting.

This is an ongoing offer, you may take advantage of it as often as you like. Do not tear this token out, just show us your copy of the book.

Canalside Craft Centre

A charming converted stone farm building, Serving meals, home made cakes tea & coffee along side a wide selection of craft gifts, books & cards, maps etc.
Outdoor seating beside the canal.

Situated in the country with woodland walks close bye. This is an area of outstanding natural beauty. **Hawthorns Park** caters for both touring and static caravans, with a designated area for tents as well. There are many facilities on site including a children's play area. Local activities include fishing, riding, climbing, walking and potholing. Plus many interesting and beautiful places to visit.

Cut out this coupon and give it to us at the time of paying and we will reduce the charge by £1.00.

Waters Edge Caravan Park offer luxury shower block, pool room, licenced lounge bar, pool room, TV room, shop, level hard standing with electric. Please ring 01539 567708 for colour brochure

---

This token entitles you to a discount of 10% off one nights accommodation and breakfast for all members of your party.

We offer a warm welcome at Primrose Cottage, Tebay, Cumbria. Leave the M6 at exit 38, Right at the roundabout and it is the first house on the right, just 400 yds. off! Offering good parking, quiet countryside and close to a good pub.

Upon receipt of this token We shall be delighted to serve you with two main courses and not charge you for the least expensive one.

The Hilcroft Hotel

Equidistant between Edinburgh and Glasgow. Ideal for business or pleasure. A privately owned modern 30 bedroomed hotel 2 Restaurants & a bar All rooms with private facilities, tea/coffee, TV, Radio, trouser press. Full Scottish breakfast.

The Hilcroft Hotel.

Equidistant between Edinburgh and Glasgow. Ideal for business or pleasure. A privately owned modern 30 bedroomed hotel. 2 Restaurants & a bar All rooms with private facilities, tea/coffee, TV, Radio, trouser press. Full Scottish breakfast.

We shall be delighted to deduct at 10% discount from the cost of your accommodation when you present this token,

---

Jonathan and Sandra Sida welcome you to
THE GREEN MAN.

We serve traditional Ridley Ales & a wide variety of delicious, well presented, homemade meals including a good selection of vegetarian dishes and a variety of children's choices. Do visit us & find out more.

WE ALREADY OFFER EXCELLENT VALUE FOR MONEY AND IF YOU SHOW US THIS ADVERTISEMENT WE WILL DEDUCT 10% FROM YOUR BILL FOR ALL FOOD SERVED.

The Red Lion

The building, originally a medieval monastery, now an 18 bedroom hotel, with bar and restaurant facilities. Away from the main road you are surrounded by history. Carved beams, log fires and cheerful staff combine to make this a very pleasant stopping off point either for an overnight stay or just a pleasant lunch or dinner break.

Show us this book when you order one or more meals over £5 and we will be pleased to serve you with FREE Tea or Coffee.

Warren Cottage Hotel,
136 The Street, Willesborough, Ashford, Kent. TN24 0NB
17th C. Hotel & Restaurant.

3 crown Commended by South East Tourist Board & English Tourist Board. Situated close to Ashford international station, the Channel Tunnel & Ferry Ports. A comfortable and friendly private hotel.

Show us this copy of "just Off..." and we will provide free tea or coffee with every meal costing over £10.

If you present this token we will discount your bill for accommodation by 10%

Watlington is considered to be the smallest town in England and **The Fox & Hounds** has been serving the towns folk for 200 years and more. Nowadays, after major refurbishment we offer **B&B**, an excellent and extensive menu, morning coffee. Just 3 miles off the motorway a warm welcome awaits.

Please present this token at reception or in the restaurant and we shall be pleased to deduct 10%

Featherstone Farm Hotel and the King's Repose Restaurant are beautifully restored ancient buildings standing in 5 acres of unspoiled countryside.

Privately managed, the service, surroundings, menus and accommodation are all presented to the highest of standards and there is a walled car park with security lighting.

CHESTNUT HOUSE HOTEL,

Great North Rd Darrington Pontefract, W Yorkshire.
At the Chestnut House Hotel we pride ourselves on excellent home cooked meals at very competitive prices. We believe we have achieved this, as we are a family run and owned business, which has been in the catering trade for over 25 years.
OPEN Monday - Saturday, 11.30-2pm & 7-9pm.
Sun. All day 11.30-8.30pm
Sorry Monday is our day of rest !
Tel. 01977 600046.

Present this token when you order your meal & we will give you a cup of tea or coffee with each main course ordered.

The Butterchurn is open 7 days a week from 10 am - 5.30pm (8.30pm on Fri/Sat/Sun.) We have a craft shop, and also sell home baking and preserves in our shop.

Brewers Fayre

...........is the Country's largest, most popular informal family pub restaurant chain. Each one offers the very best in traditional pub hospitality, with a wide range of features and facilities suitable to the whole family - from tiny tots to grandparents !

Most outlets have disabled facilities, and offer non smoking dining areas. Look out for daily specials, individually prepared by each Brewers Fayre.

When it comes to desserts, few can resist our tempting array of sweets, gateaux, hot puddings and real dairy ice creams.

Every *Brewers Fayre* is open all day every day, offering a wide choice of great value, tasty meals and snacks from 11.30 am - 10pm. (Sundays from 12noon - 10pm).

We have arranged some special vouchers offering tremendous discount - more reason to visit *Brewers Fayre !* Please tear out the voucher and present at the food till when you order your meal.

More about
Brewers Fayre.......

Families are made especially welcome at *Brewers Fayre*. Parents can relax, knowing that the facilities provided are truly welcoming. All **Brewers Fayres** provide nappy changing facilities, high chairs and a children's menu. Many have baby feeding areas and children's internal and external playing areas.

In many or our larger family pubs, there is the unique **Charlie Chalk Fun Factory** - a large self-contained area full of the latest toys, games and adventure equipment... the ultimate in FUN for kids   (small admission fee charged. Age/Height restrictions may apply – please check with the pub manager).

Family Welcome